- Excl Spreadsheet monthy income & projected /actual solutions.

exp.

40lk
ROTh IRA. (M.fund)

Operations Rules

Operations Rules

Delivering Customer Value through Flexible Operations

David Simchi-Levi

The MIT Press
Cambridge, Massachusetts
London, England

For information about special quantity discounts, please email special_sales@ mitpress.mit.edu.

This book was set in Sabon by Toppan Best-set Premedia Limited. Printed and bound in the United States of America.

Library of Congress Cataloging-in-Publication Data

Simchi-Levi, David.
Operations rules : delivering customer value through flexible operations / David Simchi-Levi.
    p.   cm.
Includes bibliographical references and index.
ISBN 978-0-262-01474-8 (hardcover : alk. paper)
1. Business logistics. 2. Operations research. 3. Consumer satisfaction. I. Title.
HD38.5.S5614 2010
658.4′034—dc22

                                                                2010008700

10   9   8   7   6   5   4   3

In memory of Dr. Michael Hammer, a colleague, a friend, and one of the most innovative thought leaders in operations

Contents

Preface

On September 22, 2008, the *Wall Street Journal* published an article called "Crude Calculations: Why High Oil Prices Are Upending the Way Companies Should Manage Their Supply Chains." This article, for which I was the lead author, grew out of my research at the Massachusetts Institute for Technology as well as collaboration with a few companies, particularly Accenture and ILOG, now part of IBM. The theme of the article, as its title suggests, was that changes in oil prices affect not only transportation costs but also almost every aspect of the supply chain.

And then a sea change occurred when the economy went into one of the biggest recessions in recent history. It was no longer just about changes in oil prices. It was also about volatile markets, declining demand, increased labor costs in developing countries, and new regulations. Change was everywhere. I realized that more than ever before, there was a need for a scientific, systematic way to help organizations manage today's challenges while preparing for tomorrow's opportunities.

The point became crystal clear in 2009 as I observed the success realized by companies that applied many of the methods and concepts discussed in this book. Unlike their competitors, these companies were able to achieve remarkable results during times of enormous challenges. I am grateful to these companies and their innovative managers and executives for the insights they provided into successful operations strategies.

It is my pleasure to thank those with whom I collaborated: Narendra Mulani, Bill Read, Jonathan Wright, and Amit Gupta (Accenture); Lance Solomon (Cisco); Annette Clayton (Dell); Sabine Müller (DHL); Jeffrey Tew (General Motors); Prashant Prabhu (Michelin); and Paul Hamilton and Tim Russell (Pepsi Bottling Group).

I received detailed feedback from many individuals. These include Rob York (Apple), Philip Roizin (Brookstone), Vah Erdekian (Cisco and MIT), Bruce Raven (Dell), Michael Romeri (Emptoris), Yih-Long Chang (Georgia Tech, College of Management), Zeynep Ton (Harvard Business School), Stephen Chick (INSEAD), Thomas J. Allen (Sloan School of Management, Massachusetts Institute of Technology), Ananth Iyer (Krannert School of Management, Purdue University), and Sherry R. Gordon (Value Chain Group).

I am grateful to the Massachusetts Institute of Technology and ILOG, now part of IBM, who provided me with the opportunity to interact with some of the brightest minds in our field. A few people stand out in this regard: Professors Charles H. Fine and Stephen C. Graves (MIT), with whom I have closely collaborated in the last ten years; my research assistant, Mohit Puri, who provided data and analysis to assess and backup some of my ideas; Derek Nelson (IBM), who tested and implemented many of the concepts that I developed in the last five years; and Pierre Haren, ILOG former CEO, with whom I spent many hours discussing topics related to this book.

Parts of this book are based on two other books I have coauthored— *The Logic of Logistics*, written with Xin Chen and Julien Bramel (second edition published by Springer in 2004), and *Designing and Managing the Supply Chain,* written with Philip Kaminsky and Edith Simchi-Levi (third edition published by McGraw-Hill in 2007).

Figures 3.1, 3.2, 3.3, 3.4, 4.1, 5.1, 5.3, 5.4, 6.1, 6.2, 6.3, 6.4, 9.1, 9.2, 9.3, 10.1, and 10.2 are, by permission, from D. Simchi-Levi, P. Kaminski and E. Simchi-Levi, *Designing and Managing the Supply Chain*, third edition © 2007 The McGraw-Hill Companies, Inc. McGraw-Hill is not responsible for the accuracy of this material.

Finally, I owe the deepest gratitude to my wife and business partner, Edith Simchi-Levi. She has been a source of support, an adviser at each stage in this project, and a reviewer of every chapter. Without her, many of the ideas and concepts described in the book would not have matured and clarified to their current level.

Operations Rules

1

The Value of Operations

In early 2005, Pepsi Bottling Group (PBG) approached the Massachusetts Institute of Technology (MIT) with a daunting challenge: consumer preference was shifting from carbonated drinks to noncarbonated drinks and from cans to bottles. At that time, PBG produced these newly preferred products in a limited number of plants, resulting in half of the plants operating at capacity and leading to service problems during periods of peak demand.[1] What did PBG do to address the problem? Did it invest in more manufacturing capacity or outsourced production? Not even close!

MIT-PBG's approach to the challenge was surprisingly simple. It focused on a flexible manufacturing strategy that matched production sourcing decisions with consumer preferences on a quarterly basis. In this strategy, quarterly sourcing decisions are based on total supply chain costs including manufacturing, transportation, and warehousing costs as well as customer service requirements. This strategy, which emphasizes cost, service, and customer preferences, improved supply chain performance by significantly reducing out-of-stock levels, effectively adding one and a half production lines' worth of capacity to PBG's supply chain without any capital expenditure.[2]

The PBG story would be incomplete if we did not mention how the new strategy affected a potentially catastrophic supply disruption. In August 2005, a fire at a Detroit chemical plant near one of PBG's suppliers threatened to shut down PBG plants, which would have led to significant financial losses. Within twenty-four hours, PBG identified lower-cost alternative production sites and prevented a supply disruption, demonstrating the power of its supply chain flexibility.[3]

Other companies have not been as successful as PBG in coping with supply disruptions or operational problems. Consider, for example, Foxmeyer, which began the year 1996 as the second-largest wholesale drug distributor in the United States (with $5 billion in revenue) and ended it with the sale of its main operating division to its largest competitor, McKesson (for $80 million). The problem was the implementation of a new information system and automated distribution center that did not work but instead created a snowball of operational problems. As if this were not enough, cost savings built into client contracts based on anticipated efficiency gains from the new systems did not materialize and generated huge financial losses.[4]

Undoubtedly, operational or supply problems can affect stock prices and shareholder wealth many months after the initial disruption. In this respect, the Mattel product recall of August 2007 is a tale worth telling. Over a period of two weeks, Mattel, the world's largest toy maker, recalled 18 million toys made in China because of hazards such as lead paint.[5] Figure 1.1 shows the five-year performance of one dollar invested in 2003 in Mattel and its competitor, Hasbro. Although both stocks moved in parallel from the third quarter of 2003 up to August of 2007,

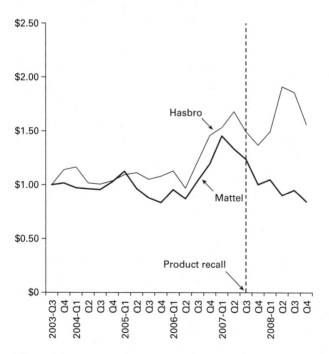

Figure 1.1
Supply chain disruption and stock performance: Stock performance for Mattel and Hasbro, 2003 to 2008

Mattel's stock went into a free fall after its recall announcement and had not recovered even a year after the disruption.

These stories are at the heart of this book. Without question, they demonstrate a link between a company's value proposition and operations strategy. The book, however, is not on any one company. Rather, it is about the *link between the customer value proposition and operations strategy* and the *principles, frameworks, and processes that allow companies to align the two while addressing today's business challenges.*

Although there are no guarantees that firms adopting these principles will always outperform the competition or will be able to overcome any source of risk, following these important principles and frameworks *significantly increases the likelihood of success.* Indeed, many of the principles and methods described in this book were implemented in numerous projects that I have been involved in, either as an adviser or as a member of the implementation team. These experiences, which allowed me to observe the successful transformation of many organizations, are the origin of the book.

1.1   Today's Business Challenges

Operations and supply chain pundits have long emphasized the importance of strategies such as just-in-time, lean manufacturing, off-shoring, and frequent deliveries to retail outlets. However, with the recent changes in the global economy, rising labor costs in developing countries, and huge volatility in oil and other commodity prices, some of these strategies may imperil the firm's supply chain and its ability to compete successfully.

For example, in the current economy, companies face an unprecedented level of volatility in demand forecast, commodity prices, and exchange rates that threatens their ability to control operations costs. Consider, for example, figure 1.2, which shows the number of days that the price of oil changed by 5 percent or more. As you can see, in normal years, the daily oil price changed by at least 5 percent only 5 to 20 times. But in 2008 it changed 39 times—definitely not a normal year! That year was the most volatile year since the recession of 1990.

The effect of oil-price volatility and upward trend—between January 2009 and January 2010, oil price increased by almost 90 percent—is exacerbated by changes in labor costs in developing countries. Between 2003 and 2008, labor costs in developing countries increased

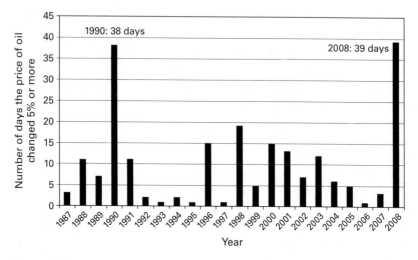

Figure 1.2
Oil price volatility, 1987 to 2008. *Source: New York Times*

Table 1.1
Average annual wage increases in five countries, 2003 to 2008

	Brazil	China	Malaysia	Mexico	United States
Average annual wage increase	21%	19%	8%	5%	3%

Source: A. Goel, N. Moussavi, and V. N. Sriatsan, "Time to Rethink Offshoring?," *McKinsey Quarterly* (September 2008).

significantly (table 1.1), much faster than the increase in labor costs in the United States or Mexico. During this period, average annual wages increased in the United States by 3 percent, in Mexico by 5 percent, and in China by 19 percent. These wage differences and the changes in oil prices suggest that off-shoring and outsourcing decisions that were made a few years ago may not be appropriate in the current environment.

At the same time, low-cost country sourcing strategies and lean practices have helped companies reduce costs but have significantly increased exposure to all sorts of risks, from operational problems to man-made and natural disasters. Similarly, globalization has increased the risk of counterfeit components and products entering the supply chain with severe consequences to the economy, public health and safety, and national security. Finally, new and future regulations around low carbon manufacturing and logistics activities may pose enormous challenges to overcome if business is to contribute to the sustainability agenda.

Interestingly, in the last few years, sustainable and green supply chains have increased in importance because of financial incentives in Europe, expected new regulations in the United States, demanding customers and supply chain partners, and the relationship between carbon footprint and supply chain efficiency. Indeed, manufacturing related logistics is a large and growing emitter of carbon dioxide that contributes about 5.5 percent of the total greenhouse gas emissions generated by human activities. Of that figure, transportation is responsible for 89 percent, and warehouses and distribution facilities are responsible for the rest. And logistics is only one—not necessarily the largest—contributor of greenhouse gas during the product lifecycle. Manufacturing, for example, contributes around 18 percent of the total greenhouse gas emissions.

With all these challenges, it is no longer clear how companies should design, manage, and operate their supply chains. Equally important, it is not obvious what the relationship should be between a company's customer value proposition and its operations strategies.

1.2   The Need to Focus

Consider Zara, the large Spanish clothing company known for fashion, stylish designs, and product diversity. Since 1974, when Amancio Ortega Gaona, Zara's chair, opened his first store, the company's objectives have been to provide customers with trendy fashion products at a reasonable, not necessarily low, price. These goals require a business model that is quite different from Zara's competitors, such as Gap Inc., one of the world's largest specialty retailers.

While retailers such as Gap reduce costs by outsourcing manufacturing (mostly to Asia), Zara owns its entire supply chain—from manufacturing through distribution centers to retail outlets. Because of its focus on fashionable, trendy products, for which demand is highly uncertain, Zara procures capacity from its fabric suppliers but does not commit necessarily to a specific color or print until it has a clear picture of consumers' preferences. Retail stores provide direct feedback to the company headquarter through its information technology (IT) infrastructure, allowing designers to identify trends and new styles.

Using this strategy, Zara has reduced time to market for new styles to three to four weeks, significantly shorter than the competition has been able to achieve. In comparison, Gap's focus on low-cost

Table 1.2
Five ways to compete in the market

Customer Value Proposition	Example	Operations Strategy
High fashion content at a reasonable price	Zara	Speed to market
Customer experience	Dell Direct	Responsiveness through configure-to-order
Product innovation	Apple	Efficiency through outsourced manufacturing and logistics
Everyday low pricing	Wal-Mart	Cost efficiency
Product selection and availability	Amazon	Efficient and reliable order fulfillment

manufacturing in Asia implies a long pipeline that is typically loaded with inventory and hence diminishes the company's ability to frequently introduce new products to the market.

The stories of Zara and Gap communicate a powerful message. Firms operating in the same space but providing different customer value propositions need different operations and supply chain strategies. Gap's focus on competitive pricing demands an operations strategy that is dedicated to efficiency—that is, a strategy where the primary goal is *reducing operational costs.* By contrast, Zara's value proposition, which provides customers with trendy fashion products at affordable prices, requires an operations strategy that is focused on speed—that is, a strategy where a vertically integrated supply chain is dedicated to *responsiveness.*

To highlight the strong connection between customer value proposition and its related operations strategies, consider five Fortune 500 companies: Zara, Dell Direct, Apple, Wal-Mart, and Amazon (table 1.2). Every one of these five companies has had superior financial performance over a long period of time, each provides a unique value proposition, and each company's operations strategy directly matches its customer value proposition.

Dell outperformed the competition by over 3,000 percent in share-holder growth from 1988 to 1996.[6] Dell's success over this eight-year period can be attributed to its virtual integration, a strategy that blurs the traditional boundaries between suppliers, manufacturers, and end users. Dell's decision to sell computers built from components produced by other manufacturers relieved the firm of the burden of owning assets, investing in research and development, and managing a large workforce. At the same time, its direct sales model allows consumers to configure their own computers and requires Dell to fully customize an order with a short response time.

Dell's recent struggles are in part due to a change in the personal computer market. Growth in the PC market has shifted from online to retail and from developed countries to emerging markets, where consumers are not used to or not comfortable with online purchasing. Such a shift requires a rethinking of operations and supply chain strategies. Indeed, the frameworks developed in this book show that Dell's responsive configure-to-order strategy is a mismatch with the characteristics of the retail channel.

Apple, another example from table 1.2, has outsourced almost all its PC manufacturing and logistics activities. The firm focuses mainly on research, development, and product innovation as well as marketing and sales. Apple's product portfolio, unlike Dell's, is limited and hence its operations strategy emphasizes efficiency rather than responsiveness. For this purpose, Apple serves as the supply chain coordinator, integrator, and provider of operations best-practices, innovations, and strategies for all its partners.

Finally, Amazon and Wal-Mart are direct competitors in the retail space, each of which focuses on a different channel and a different value proposition. Amazon, the world's largest Internet retailer, provides its customers with a huge variety of products—including books, DVDs, electronics, and other merchandise—and has established itself as the most trusted online retailer through an efficient and reliable order-fulfillment strategy. By contrast, Wal-Mart has built its reputation as the brick-and-mortar master retailer by focusing on squeezing cost and increasing efficiency in its supply chain, thus providing its customers with competitive pricing but not necessarily with extraordinary service.

Looking at the customer value propositions and the corresponding operations strategies for these successful companies reveals an important insight: No firm can compete successfully on all dimensions of customer value, such as innovation, choice, price, and experience. Management needs to pick its goals, since operations and supply chain strategies, the market channel, or even the skill sets required to be successful depend on the specific value proposition.[7]

Similarly, no firm can be both extremely efficient, and thus compete on price, and at the same time highly responsive, and thus provide its customers with a large set of choices in a speedy manner while maintaining an extraordinary service level. These are conflicting objectives, an issue that is discussed in the next section.

1.3   The Challenge

Traditional operations strategies have often focused on efficiency or responsiveness or a combination of the two. In operational efficiency, the firm focuses on low-cost strategies across all functional areas. This includes supplier selection, manufacturing, product design, and distribution and logistics. Typically, in such a strategy, production and distribution decisions are based on long-term forecasts, inventory of finished goods is positioned close to market demand, and supplier selection is based mostly on component costs. Hence, sourcing from low-cost countries is often the mantra.

By contrast, a responsive strategy focuses on speed, order fulfillment, service level, and customer satisfaction. Here, the objective is not necessarily to squeeze as much cost out of the supply chain as is humanly possible but rather to eliminate stockouts and satisfy demand by competing on response time and speed to market. Typically, in such a strategy, product variety is high and product lifecycle is short, manufacturing or product assembly is based on realized demand rather than forecast, products may be customized, a buffer inventory of components is emphasized, and sourcing, supplier selection, and transportation strategies all rely on speed rather than only on low cost.

Although seasoned operations and supply chain executives understand the difference between efficiency and responsiveness, many are confused about when to apply each strategy. Worse still! Senior managers typically spend a considerable amount of time and energy on customer value but may be ignorant about the connection between the consumer value proposition and operations strategies.

At the heart of the problem is the question "What drives operations and supply chain strategies?" The research reported in this book shows that the customer value proposition, channels to market, and product characteristics are the key drivers of an appropriate operations strategy. Implementing a strategy that does not match these drivers leads to inefficiencies, unnecessary expenses, and poor customer service at best or to an eventual business failure in the worst case.

Even those who understand the need to match operations strategies with the drivers reported above are faced with three independent challenges. The first is the existence of mismatches between the strategies

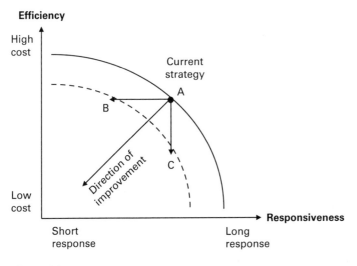

Figure 1.3
Trade-offs between efficiency and responsiveness

suggested by different product characteristics. That is, managers often find that some product attributes push the operations strategy in one direction while other attributes pull the strategy in a different direction.

The second challenge exists after identifying the appropriate strategy. At that time, executives often discover that different products, channels, or even customers require different types of supply chains. Thus, they need to decide whether operations should establish a single supply chain and, if so, which one. If multiple supply chains are required, should these supply chains operate independently, or is there a way to take advantage of synergies across the various supply chains?

The third challenge emerges as executives grasp for a better understanding of the drivers of their operations strategy. Operations affect three measures of performance: cost, time, and service levels. Unfortunately, these are conflicting objectives, as is illustrated in figure 1.3, where the solid curve represents trade-offs between efficiency and responsiveness. This curve, sometimes referred to as the *efficient frontier,* represents a range of possible strategies, each with a corresponding cost (efficiency) and response time (responsiveness). Indeed, a high efficiency level, that is, a low-cost operations strategy, typically increases time to serve customers and does not emphasize a high level of service. Alternatively, a highly responsive strategy increases cost but reduces customer response time.

Taken together, the three challenges impose enormous barriers for managers looking for strategies that differentiate them from the competition and create a sustainable competitive advantage. Addressing these challenges requires a shift from best practice to a more systematic and scientific approach that links customer value, product characteristics, and market channels directly with operations strategy.

The term *best practice* refers to the achievement of a specific outcome—higher level of service, lower cost, shorter response time, or any other performance measure—by following accepted management principles. For example, best practice led a major supplier in the automotive industry to invest in demand forecasting technology and associated processes to reduce inventory levels. The intuition is clear: accurate forecasts reduce safety stock and hence overall inventory. But as appealing as it was, the forecast improvement had no significant impact on this supplier's inventory levels. At the heart of the inventory crisis the company was facing was not poor forecast accuracy—as suggested by accepted management principles—but rather a poor choice of where inventory was positioned in the supply chain. Repositioning stock led to a 30 percent reduction in inventory levels while maintaining the same level of service and response time.

This story suggests that there is a need for deeper understanding of what drives operations strategy. For this purpose, the book converts ideas, observations, and research into a set of rules that management can follow to achieve a quantum leap in operations performance. These rules, which I refer to as the *engineering of operations and supply chains,* are at the heart of powerful frameworks that allow executives to *match strategies with customer value propositions, channels, and product characteristics.*

Ignore these rules, and you will find yourself heading toward failure. Follow them, and you will steer yourself away from predictable problems and toward an operations strategy that drives real business value.

1.4   Trade-offs and Rules

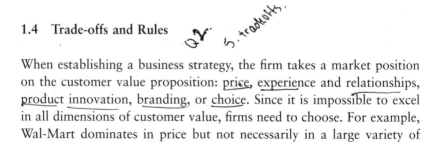

When establishing a business strategy, the firm takes a market position on the customer value proposition: price, experience and relationships, product innovation, branding, or choice. Since it is impossible to excel in all dimensions of customer value, firms need to choose. For example, Wal-Mart dominates in price but not necessarily in a large variety of products, while Amazon dominates in choice and product availability but not necessarily in price.

A business strategy thus characterizes a company's unique position in the market and distinguishes the firm's value proposition from that of its competitors. Such a unique market position drives and depends on operations and supply chain strategies. Unfortunately, no company can be both highly efficient (delivering low cost) and extremely responsive (delivering short response times and dazzling customer satisfaction). This is where the need to make trade-offs emerges.

Of course, trade-offs need to be made not only between efficiency and responsiveness but also between flexibility and cost, cost and exposure to risk, inventory and service levels, and between quality and price. Each of these trade-offs entails a diagram similar to figure 1.3.

Operations and supply chain innovation is about improving performance despite these trade-offs. Consider figure 1.3, and assume that your current strategy corresponds to point A on the solid efficient frontier curve. This strategy invests in a deliberate trade-off between efficiency and responsiveness.

Imagine now that you devise a new strategy that somehow pushes the efficient frontier downward. If this is possible, then for the same level of efficiency, you can improve response time (point B). Alternatively, for the same level of responsiveness, you can improve operations efficiency and hence reduce costs (point C). More importantly, there is a range of strategies between B and C where the firm improves both efficiency and responsiveness.

This insight is the motivation behind many of the rules and associated concepts featured in this book. Indeed, they enable this shift in the trade-off curve. Examples include the concept of push-pull (chapter 3), risk sharing contracts (chapter 4), process and technology integration (chapter 6), and flexibility (chapters 7, 8, and 9).

This is the essence of PBG's newly established operations strategy. Prior to collaborating with MIT, PBG focused on supply chain efficiency. But faced with shifts in consumer preference, PBG needed a new approach that eliminated the stockout crises the firm faced during periods of peak demand but that did not increase and in fact even decreased supply chain costs. Thus, PBG was not trying to move along its existing efficient frontier but rather push its efficient frontier downward and thereby eliminate stockouts and decrease costs.

Other rules are designed to help companies match operations strategy with product characteristics, channels, and customer value. Examples include rules regarding channels, price, product characteristics, and value-added services (chapter 2), procurement-strategy rules (chapter 4), and rules associated with IT strategy (chapter 6).

The origin of all the rules in this book is scientific. They are all based on either mathematical or empirical approaches. By *mathematical*, I refer to rules derived from detailed mathematical models. These rules are universal laws that are always true, independent of geography, culture, or products. Examples include principles that govern the relationships between variability and supply chain performance, between inventory, capacity, and response time, between redundancy and supply chain cost, and between information, lead time, and variability.

The empirical approach devises rules based on carefully conducted research that observes the strategies and performance of various companies. Such rules are also universal, but like any empirical research, and unlike mathematical models, they need to be considered within the context of the origin of the data. Examples include principles that explain the relationships between operations strategies and channel characteristics, product attributes, customer value, and IT capability.

Together, the two approaches complement each other and generate a set of principles that transform operations and supply chain management from a discipline that is based on gut feelings, anecdotes, and best practice to a true engineering discipline.

1.5   The Journey Ahead

The book includes three interrelated parts. Part I (chapters 2–6) presents an analytical framework for understanding operations strategy. Part II (chapters 7–9) outlines an implementation framework for a key supply chain enabler, flexibility, the single most important capability that enables the firm to innovate its operations and supply chain strategies. Finally, Part III (chapters 10 and 11) discusses emerging trends that are likely to stir profound changes in operations and supply chain strategies. The book concludes with a chapter on the barriers to success in operations (chapter 12).

Operations Strategy

Operations strategy is an important enabler of the business strategy. To characterize the link between the two, the firm's customer value proposition—the unique market position that the firm defines in its business strategy—needs to be examined in depth. Chapter 2 identifies the dimensions that define customer value and characterizes properties that affect operations and supply chain strategies. Chapter 3 builds on these properties and develops a framework that enables matching products and markets with supply chain strategies.

Chapter 4 takes a step further in analyzing the gap between management objectives of procuring high-quality products at the lowest possible total cost of ownership and the reality that most companies' cost to procure is higher than expected, procurement savings are lower than anticipated, and the procurement organization is typically considered inefficient. I argue that the origin of this gap is a misalignment between the firm's value proposition and the procurement strategy. Too often, procurement marches to its own drum independently of operations or business strategy. To address this challenge, chapter 4 develops a framework that links the customer value proposition with the procurement strategy while addressing both supply and price risks. Of course, managing price and supply risks is only part of the broader challenge of managing risk in the supply chain. A failure to manage risk can wipe out an entire organization. Hence, chapter 5 explores rules and principles that can be applied to mitigate man-made and natural sources of risks.

This part of the book ends in chapter 6 with a discussion of information technology. The starting point is the link between business strategies and IT investments. This link, established by analyzing core operational capabilities that IT supports, provides valuable insights into IT investment decisions. I argue that although IT is becoming a commodity that is available to any organization, it is its combination with business processes that enables competitive advantage.

Flexibility

The second part of the book digs deeper into a key concept in operations strategy—flexibility. As is illustrated in chapters 3, 4, and 5, flexibility can be a powerful tool for gaining competitive advantage, reducing costs, and improving responsiveness. At the heart of established business strategies, such as Toyota's lean manufacturing, Dell's direct-to-consumer model, and PBG's recent success story, is a flexible operation that is designed to match the firm's business model and customer value proposition.

So what exactly is flexibility? In chapter 7, *flexibility* is defined as "the ability to respond to change without increasing operational and supply chain costs and with little or no delay in response time." In this definition, *change* refers to change in demand volume and mix, commodity prices, labor costs, exchange rates, technology, equipment availability, production processes, the logistics environment, or any other conditions in the market.

How can a firm achieve flexibility? In this book, the different strategies that have been applied to achieve flexibility are classified into three categories: system design, process design, and product design.

System design (chapter 7)   Firms can achieve flexibility through manufacturing or distribution strategy or through capacity redundancy.

Process design (chapter 8)   Examples of achieving flexibility through process design include a flexible workforce, worker cross-training, a lean manufacturing, organization and management structure, and varied procurement strategies such as flexible contracts, dual sourcing and outsourcing.

Product design (chapter 9)   Design solutions that allow a firm to achieve flexibility include modular product architecture, standard components and interfaces, postponement strategies, and component substitution.

Emerging Trends

The final part of the book addresses two important trends that have emerged in the last few years—oil-price volatility (chapter 10) and corporate social responsibility (chapter 11). Oil price has been on a roller-coaster ride in recent years and this volatility and upward trend has affected supply chain strategies.

Similarly, pressured by governments, customers, and trading partners, some senior managers has started focusing on corporate social responsibility, particularly as it relates to the effect of their supply chains on the environment. But corporate social responsibility is not only about striving for a greener supply chain. It also encompasses the range of decisions that provide social and environmental benefits. Unfortunately, most senior managers consider corporate social responsibility to be a form of charity, philanthropy, or mere compliance with regulations. But nothing is further from the truth. In an economy with an overabundance of supply and with many products that are viewed as interchangeable commodities, corporate social responsibility offers an opportunity for new revenue streams, additional efficiencies, and unique branding.

The book concludes with a review of the barriers to success as a way to reinforce the themes in the book.

Notes

1. A. Ackerman and A. Padilla, "Pepsi Bottling Group Achieves Optimization Success," 2009, available at http://www.consumergoods.com (accessed on December 23, 2009).

2. D. Simchi-Levi, T. Russell, B. Charles, T. McLoughlin, and P. Hamilton, "Case Study: Transforming Production Sourcing at Pepsi Bottling Group," White Paper, IBM and PBG, November 2009.

3. T. Russell, "Production Sourcing at PBG," Paper presented at the ILOG Supply Chain Symposium, September 2007.

4. "The Greatest Supply Chain Disasters of All Time," *Supply Chain Digest* (May 2009).

5. "Mattel shares tumble on another global recall of toys made in China," *Financial Times*, August 15, 2007.

6. D. Simchi-Levi, P. Kaminsky, and E. Simchi-Levi, *Designing and Managing the Supply Chain: Concepts, Strategies, and Case Studies,* 3rd ed. (New York: McGraw-Hill, 2007).

7. A similar observation on customer value proposition is made in F. Crawford and R. Mathews, *The Myth of Excellence* (New York: Crown Business, 2001).

I

Operations Strategy

2

From Customer Value to Operations Strategy

In today's customer-driven markets, what matters most is not the product or service but rather the customer's perceived value of the entire relationship with a company. In the last few years, many companies have emphasized both the quality of their products and services and customer satisfaction, which involves understanding current customers, their use of the products, and their impression of the company's service. The emphasis on customer value goes a step further by establishing the reasons that a customer chooses a specific product and by analyzing the entire range of products, services, and intangibles that constitute the company's image and brand—including, in many cases, its stand on social and environmental issues.

This focus on customer value promotes a broader look at a company's offerings and its customers. It requires understanding why customers purchase, continue to purchase, or defect from a company. What are their preferences and needs, and how can they be satisfied? Which customers are profitable and have potential for revenue growth, and which customers may lead to losses?

Assumptions about customer value need to be examined carefully to ensure an accurate understanding of what drives demand. Some examples of questions that must be asked include the following:

· Does the customer value low prices, superior quality, or excellent customer support services?
· Does the customer prefer next day delivery or many choices?
· Does the customer prefer to purchase from a specialized store or from a megastore that provides one-stop shopping opportunities?
· Does the customer prefer choosing from a large menu of similar items or a fixed, small menu of low-price products?

These are critical questions for any business and should be the driving force behind business strategy and performance measures. The answers to these questions can help determine an appropriate operations strategy.

Evidently, the operations strategy that should be employed when customers value price is different from the strategy that should be employed when customers value choice—a large menu of similar items—or when service and response times are critical. Similarly, if customers value one-stop shopping, companies may have to carry a large number of products and options, even at the expense of high inventory levels. Therefore, the supply chain needs to be considered in any product, sales, and business strategy and could, in itself, provide a competitive advantage leading to increased customer value and eventually to business growth.

Consider Dell's direct-to-consumer business model versus Hewlett-Packard's retail strategy. In Dell's business model, customer experience is the value proposition, so Dell deploys an assemble-to-order strategy that enables each consumer to configure his or her own product from a large menu of options. By contrast, the retail strategy employed by HP focuses on a limited number of configurations but emphasizes a competitive pricing strategy, and so it must be supported by a supply chain whose focus is on cost and efficiency.

The downfall of Kmart, to give another example, is attributed in part to a supply chain strategy that was not consistent with its business value proposition—a value proposition centered around competing with Wal-Mart on price. Since the early 1980s, Wal-Mart's goal has been to provide customers with access to goods when and where they want them and to develop a cost structure that enables competitive pricing. The key to achieving this goal has been to make the supply chain the centerpiece of its strategy. Indeed, Wal-Mart has been able to lower costs by introducing the cross-docking strategy, engaging in strategic partnering with its suppliers, and investing in information technology that connects tightly with its suppliers. By contrast, Kmart's strong desire to keep earnings discouraged investments in supply chain efficiencies and information technology. By the late 1990s, it became clear that Kmart's supply chain was not as efficient as Wal-Mart's and as a result could not compete on price.[1]

These stories about Dell, Hewlett-Packard, Wal-Mart, and Kmart provide an important lesson:

Rule 2.1   *The operations strategy that a company deploys must be driven by the value proposition that the firm provides to its customers.*

This rule, then, must be at the heart of any corporate discussion regarding its operations strategy. Hence, before we identify the appropriate operations strategy, it is essential to define the customer value proposition provided by the firm.

I define *customer value* as "the way customers perceive the company's offerings, including products, services, and other intangibles." Customers' perceptions can have several dimensions:

- Product innovation,
- Product selection and availability,
- Price and brand,
- Value-added services, and
- Relationships and experiences.

The first three items in this list of dimensions are the essentials, and the final two items are more sophisticated dimensions that may not always be as important but can be mined for ideas to create a unique way to add value and differentiation to a company's offering.

Taking a position along each one of the customer value dimensions defines the business strategy. In this chapter, I examine each dimension and its impact on operations challenges and business strategy.

2.1 Product Innovation

There is no doubt that designing products to match customer requirements is key to market success. But *product characteristics* can refer to many different aspects of product features and design. So what characteristics are important and relevant to the discussion about operations strategy?

A careful observation of effective operations and supply chain strategies for various physical products—such as apparel, PCs, automotive products, and consumer packaged goods—suggests a striking insight. *Product innovation speed*—sometimes referred to as *technology* or *product clock speed*[2]—that is, the speed by which technologies or products change in a particular industry, fundamentally and dramatically affects operations strategy. To understand the impact, we relate the innovation speed to two product types—functional products and innovative products.[3]

Functional products are characterized by slow innovation speed, low product variety, and typically low profit margins. Examples include grocery products (such as milk, soap, and flour), car tires, and basic office equipment. *Innovative products* are characterized by fast technology innovation speed, short product life cycle, high product variety, and relatively high margins. Examples include fashion items and electronics.

Often, the same product can be both functional and innovative. Basic food products—such as pasta, coffee, and jam—are offered in standard packaging as well as in artisanal or gourmet options. Similarly, the same company, for instance Tommy Hilfiger, manufactures products that are functional—white button-down shirts—and fashionable, as in its latest fall designs.

Undoubtedly, the supply chain strategy for innovative products—products and industries where the products or technology change frequently—must be fundamentally different than that for slow innovation speed products. Similarly, product design strategy and its relationship with supply chain characteristics depend on product innovation speed.

Table 2.1 compares the characteristics of functional and innovative products.[4] As you can see, this distinction between innovative and functional products has an enormous effect on forecast accuracy, the risk of obsolescence, and the cost of lost sales and hence must affect the type of supply chain employed in each case.

Rule 2.2   *Functional and innovative products typically require different supply chain strategies.*

Even those who understand this rule are sometimes confused about its usefulness. First, it is indeed possible for a product to start as an innovative product and shift later in the product lifecycle to become a commodity or a functional product. Second, many products—for example, PCs, furniture, or even apparel—can be offered in different forms, either as

Table 2.1
Functional versus innovative products

	Functional	Innovative
Product variety	Low	High
Product life cycle	Long	Short
Forecast accuracy	High	Low
Risk of obsolescence	Low	High
Cost of lost sale	Low	High

functional or innovative.[5] Finally, functional and innovative products are two extreme product characteristics on a spectrum that spans various degrees of technology innovation speed. So what should a company do in these situations? What product design, supply chain, and operations strategies should be applied? These questions are answered in the next chapter.

2.2 Product Selection and Availability

Many products come in a large variety of options, styles, colors, and shapes. A car may come in five styles, ten different exterior colors, and ten interior colors and with automatic or manual transmission—a total of a thousand configurations. Typically, these products compete in the market, and while it may be easy to predict the aggregated demand level across, for example, all midsize cars, it is difficult to predict demand for a specific configuration. Such product proliferation leads to high inventory levels.

Product proliferation is also a function of the sales channel. Indeed, many online retailers have focused on providing their customers with numerous choices of similar products, while brick and mortar retailers competing in the same space offer a smaller subset of the same products. Think about the numerous possible configurations that HP offers on its Web site versus the limited options that it sells through traditional retailers such as Best Buy.

One interesting aspect of the Internet, referred to by Chris Anderson[6] as "the long tail" phenomena, occurs in the almost limitless market of supply and demand that has been opened by online retailing. In this market, the lack of physical or local restrictions allows retailers to focus on and generate significant revenue from the less popular items in their catalogs.

To illustrate this phenomenon, consider the book industry, where Amazon sells almost all the 5 million of unique title books available in print while a traditional retailer like Barnes & Noble carries only 100,000 titles.[7] This proliferation of books provides Amazon with a huge advantage. According to Anderson, 30 percent of Amazon's sales are from books that are not available in a typical retail store.

This pattern is not unique to the book industry. Consider the rental movie industry, where Netflix stocks about 90,000 unique DVDs, while a typical retail store offers a few hundred titles.[8] Nearly 95 percent of the titles offered by Netflix are rented at least once a quarter.

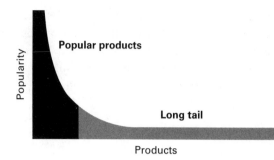

Figure 2.1
The long-tail phenomenon

Table 2.2
Retail versus online products

	Retail	Online
Product variety	Low	High
Customization	Limited	High
Forecast accuracy	High	Low
Volume by product	High	Low

This is the *long-tail phenomenon,* which is illustrated in figure 2.1. Companies such as Amazon and Netflix make between a quarter to half of their revenues on titles not carried by traditional retailers such as Wal-Mart, which carries only the most popular titles.

Of course, the long-tail phenomenon says nothing about profit margin. Indeed, while a large fraction of online revenue is generated by titles not carried by traditional retailers, this inventory can be expensive. This is true since sales volume by product for these items is low, and hence forecast accuracy is poor, leading to high safety stock. Similarly, low volume implies an inability to take advantage of economies of scale in both procurement and transportation costs. Thus, the channel significantly affects the supply chain strategy. Indeed, supply chain challenges and opportunities are quite different, depending on whether the firm sells its product online or in traditional retail stores, as is illustrated in table 2.2.

Naturally, when the online retailer sells downloadable products—such as application software, electronic books, movies, or songs—the long tail represents both revenue and profit.

Rule 2.3 *Different channels may require different supply chain strategies.*

Product selection relates directly to product availability. Amazon does not necessarily hold inventory of the very low-selling products in its portfolio—those on the far right-hand side of the tail in figure 2.1. Consequently, delivery lead time for some of the low-selling products is quite long since Amazon has to order the products from the manufacturer after receiving a customer order. But for most of its collection of products, availability and a short response time are central to Amazon's strategy.

By contrast, specialty retailers such as Zara, Saks Fifth Avenue, or Neiman Marcus offer a large selection of fashion products but emphasize scarcity, not availability, in their business strategy. By running low on inventory, these retailers shape consumers' behavior and motivate them to purchase early in the selling season rather than wait for a discount. This creates an urgency to purchase, reduces inventory, and eliminates the need for a discount—a huge problem for traditional retailers. Indeed, Zara, for example, sells about 80 to 85 percent of its products at full price compared with 60 to 70 percent for its competitors.

The downside of this business strategy is the loss of potential upside—selling more of popular products. To address this challenge, Zara emphasizes an operations strategy that is built around speed to market so that production and even product design can be delayed until market signal information is available. Store managers monitor sales and trends and make product assortment and inventory decisions in order to be responsive to local needs. This information about popular styles and trends is used to guide product design and production decisions.

Thus, Zara's time to market—from product design through manufacturing all the way to store shelves—is between two to five weeks, significantly shorter than the industry average of six months. This allows Zara to replenish stores at the beginning of and during the selling season, while most its competitors replenish only once, at the beginning of a season.

Madonna's three-week concert tour in Spain illustrates Zara's speed-to-market capability. Thanks to Zara, some members of the audience arrived to the singer's last Spanish show wearing the same outfit that she introduced in her first concert.[9]

2.3   Price and Brand

The price of products is an essential dimension of customer value. Although price may not be the only factor that a customer considers, certain products may have a narrow range of acceptable prices. For instance, for commodity products—even relatively sophisticated items such as personal computers—there is little flexibility in price, so companies achieve cost advantages through innovations in their operations.

The success story of Wal-Mart, a supply chain innovator, is well known. Its business strategy is centered on providing its customers with low-cost merchandise and thus undercutting its competition. In addition, its everyday-low-pricing (EDLP) strategy is an important tool in reducing the bullwhip effect (see appendix A). Customers do not have to worry about buying at the wrong time, and manufacturers do not need to plan for demand variations as a result of promotions.

Brand is an important factor affecting product price across a wide variety of retail environments, from auto superstores to online retailers. Consider the prices of books and CDs sold online. A study conducted in 2000, when Internet sales started taking off, found "substantial and systematic differences in price across retailers on the Internet. Prices posted on the Internet differ by an average of 33 percent for books and 25 percent for CDs." But Internet retailers with the lowest prices do not necessarily sell more products than their higher-priced competitors. For instance, the study found that Books.com had a lower price than Amazon in 99 percent of the cases studied, and yet Amazon had about 80 percent of the market at that time while Books.com had about 2 percent. One way to explain this behavior is through the "trust consumers have for various Internet retailers and the associated value of branding."[10]

Because a brand is a guarantee of quality in the buyer's mind, the Internet and its effect on consumer behavior have increased the importance of brand names. Brand names such as Mercedes cars, Rolex watches, and Coach bags can be promoted for high quality and prestige and command much higher prices than products that lack this aura. Furthermore, the higher price in itself may be a large part of the prestige and perceived quality.

Another example of the effect of brand is in the overnight-delivery market. One key driver in the rise of Federal Express as the most successful small-package carrier is that it was the first to narrow its focus to overnight delivery, thereby owning the word *overnight* in the market. Even though there are cheaper alternatives, customers are willing to pay a premium to ship by Federal Express because of the brand name and the perception of dependability that it conveys.[11]

Of course, the pricing strategy and supply chain strategy must align. A firm that competes on price needs a different supply chain strategy than the one used by a company that competes on other customer and business values. A powerful way to illustrate this point is to focus on profit margin. The smaller the profit margin—perhaps due to everyday-low-pricing strategy or operational inefficiencies—the more important it is to focus on cutting cost out of the supply chain.

To better understand the impact of profit margin, we review the financial performance of seven companies from two different industries where costs and revenues are proportional. The PC companies include ACER, Dell, Lenovo, and HP, and the companies that sell consumer packaged goods are Clorox, P&G, and Colgate. The 2008 annual reports of these companies suggest a big difference between the two industries' profit margins and a huge difference between profit margins of the four companies in the PC industry (see table 2.3).

For example, in 2008, the profit margin for Lenovo was about 9.8 percent, for HP 9.18 percent, for Dell 5.69 percent, and for ACER 2.94 percent. Clearly, reducing operating cost by one percentage point would have translated directly into bottom-line benefits (net profit). To achieve the same impact on net profit through higher sales, Lenovo would need to increase its revenue by 10.2 (= 0.01 / 0.098) percentage points, HP by 10.9, Dell by 17.6, and ACER by 34 (see table 2.3). The implications are clear: the smaller the profit margins, the more important it is to focus on reducing operating costs.

Table 2.3
The increase in revenue required to achieve the same impact as cutting cost by 1 percent

	Profit margin (2008)	Revenue increase (per 1% decrease in operating cost)
ACER	2.94%	34.0%
Dell	5.69%	17.6%
HP	9.18%	10.9%
Lenovo	9.8%	10.2%
Clorox	17.22%	5.8%
P&G	20.11%	5.0%
Colgate	20.91%	4.8%

Rule 2.4   *Competition on price requires tight control of supply chain costs.*

2.4   Value-Added Services

Many companies cannot compete on product price alone in an economy that has an overabundance of supply and includes many products that are commodities. Therefore, they need to distinguish themselves with value-added offerings that may also provide them with higher profitability.

In the last few years, business executives have come to realize that there is a limit to how much cost savings and business growth they can derive from the traditional supply chain that is responsible for their core products. These companies are now paying attention to the ability of the service-parts supply chain to add value for their customers as well as increase their revenue and profit.

Consider, for example, Mercedes-Benz's recent year-over-year sales growth in China. The 65 percent growth rate positioned the firm as the fastest growing luxury manufacturer in a very competitive, slowly growing market. Undoubtedly, this success is correlated with the firm's strategy of distinguishing itself from other luxury brands with its after-sales services. Indeed, J. D. Power Asia Pacific 2008 China Customer Satisfaction ranked the firm a strong first with 44 percent of its customers saying they would recommend their service dealer to others—compared with an industry average of about 20 percent.

One important driver in the growth of value-added services is a significant increase in information technology capabilities. IT provides almost limitless opportunities for innovative companies to interact with customers, provide them with real-time information about a required service, and sometimes replace physical products with their digital counterparts. All of these opportunities require tighter relationships between suppliers and customers, which is an important objective of most organizations.

These observations are consistent with a recent study from the Aberdeen Group, which found that after-sale services—such as repairs, upgrades, and maintenance—account for between 10 to 40 percent of the revenue of many industrial companies and drive a large portion of their inventory costs.[12] The same group estimates that both after-sale service and spare-parts management account for about 8 percent of the

Table 2.4
A traditional supply chain versus a service supply chain

	Traditional	Service
Product variety	Depends on business strategy	Always high
Response time	Days	Hours
Objective	Service level	Machine uptime
Demand characteristics	Depends on product characteristic	Sporadic and unpredictable

United States annual gross domestic products, suggesting a huge opportunity for better managing and optimizing these services.

Unfortunately, managing the after-service supply chain presents challenges that are quite different from those facing the traditional supply chain (see table 2.4).[13] As you can see, the two supply chains can differ in the number of products and in demand characteristics, and they clearly focus on different objectives and different response times. In a service supply chain, the objective is to maximize machine uptime, typically by guaranteeing a very short response time of only a few hours. In a traditional supply chain, the objective typically is a high service level or fill rate.

Rule 2.5 *Differentiation through after-sale service requires specialized supply chain capabilities.*

As is noted in later chapters, flexibility is important for traditional supply chains, but it is critical for service-parts supply chains. This is true since it is difficult to satisfy requirements such as high machine uptime and very short response time when demand is sporadic and unpredictable.

2.5   Relationships and Experiences

The final dimension of customer value is an increased connection between the firm and its customers through the development of a relationship. Since a relationship requires time investment from both the customer and the vendor, this reduces the likelihood that customers will switch to other providers.

The learning relationship—where companies build specific user profiles and use this information to enhance sales as well as retain customers[14]—is an example of a relationship providing customer value. Companies such as USAA, which uses its databases to offer customers other services and products, are examples of this kind of organization.

Some Internet sites, such as Amazon.com, have applied new modes of learning by offering suggestions to customers based on their own purchase history or the purchase history of customers with similar purchase characteristics. One issue with an Internet service that provides customer reviews and suggestions is that consumers can distinguish between a Web site where they purchase the product and the Web site in which they receive information about the product. That is, it is not clear that a Web site that provides suggestion tools and customer reviews can convince the consumer to purchase the product at that site. The consumer may well receive information from one site and make the purchase on another.[15]

An approach that was tailored to large customers and designed to make it difficult for them to switch to another vendor was introduced by Dell. It offers large corporations custom PC configurations that are loaded with specific software, tags, and other special requirements. Such a tailored solution, combined with the high volume associated with corporate orders, requires a different supply chain strategy than the one applied to serve individual consumers. To illustrate the need for a different supply chain strategy, consider table 2.5, which compares the business challenges for working with corporate clients and individual consumers.

Beyond customer relationships, some companies are also designing, promoting, and selling unique experiences to their customers. Customer experience includes all the touch points between the firm and its clients—

Table 2.5
Channel type: Corporate clients versus individual consumers

	Corporate	Individual
Product variety	Low	High
Product design for	Client	Market
Forecast accuracy	High	Low
Volume by product	High	Low
Customer relationship	Tight	Loose

from its Web site to pricing, product quality, packaging, and distribution all the way to customer service and after-sale offerings such as repairs and upgrades. The challenge is that when different people are responsible for the various touch points, they may not realize that they are part of the customer experience, or even worse, they may have a different interpretation of what the customer experience entails.[16]

The ability to provide good customer experience is very different from the ability to manage customer relationships effectively or to manufacture and distribute products successfully. To illustrate this point, think about measuring and managing *customer experience* versus *customer relationships*. The latter is typically the responsibility of customer facing teams—including sales and marketing—whereas the former involves more than customer facing teams and hence is difficult to manage or measure. Indeed, businesses typically measure customer satisfaction, not experience. Unfortunately, it is hard to deduce from information about customer satisfaction any specific insights on customer experience and the existence of a friction in the various touch points.

Finally, when a firm uses experience as a way to engage and drive consumers, it may need to adjust its operations and supply chain strategy. For example, Amazon's reputation for excellent customer experience and effective service is a result of a focus on an efficient, consistent, and reliable fulfillment strategy. For years, Amazon allowed other retailers to sell through its Web site, but customers complained about poor quality and service, which affected customer experience and drove Amazon to change its fulfillment strategy. Amazon's 2006 initiative, "Fulfillment by Amazon," requires retailers to ship products to Amazon distribution centers, and Amazon is responsible for everything else, including packaging, shipping, returns, and customer service.[17]

Rule 2.6   *Improved customer experience requires a higher level of supply chain excellence.*

2.6   Summary

In the last few years, I have observed many companies that have a mismatch between their customer value proposition and their operations strategy. In many cases, this is a result of a poor understanding of operations and supply chain strategies. In other cases, the mismatch results when the firm applies one supply chain strategy across all its market segments, even though those segments have different characteristics, and provides different value propositions.

This chapter illustrates that the firm's value proposition—including product innovation, pricing, choices and availability, experience, and relationships—affects operations strategies. The next chapter directly connects product and market characteristics with operations and supply chain strategies.

Finally, another dimension that has become increasingly important to consumers and therefore should be included in customer value is corporate social responsibility. This relates foremost to environmental issues, such as carbon emissions, recycling, packaging, and water and energy conservation. Other social topics involve community development, safety standards, and working conditions. We provide a comprehensive treatment of this aspect of customer value in chapter 11.

Notes

1. G. Stalk, P. Evans, and L. E. Shulman, "Competing on Capabilities: The New Rule of Corporate Strategy," *Harvard Business Review* (March–April 1992): 57–69; C. Sliwa, "Beyond IT: Business Strategy Was a Problem, Too," *Computerworld* (January 25, 2002).

2. C. Fine, *Clockspeed* (Reading: Perseus Books, 1998).

3. M. L. Fisher, "What Is the Right Supply Chain for Your Product?," *Harvard Business Review* (March–April 1997): 105–117.

4. Ibid.

5. Ibid.

6. C. Anderson, *The Long Tail* (New York: Hyperion Books, 2006, 2008).

7. Ibid.

8. Ibid.

9. "The Future of Fast Fashion," *The Economist* (June 16, 2005).

10. E. Brynjolfsson and M. D. Smith, "Frictionless Commerce? A Comparison of Internet and Conventional Retailers," *Management Science* 46 (2000): 563–585.

11. A. Ries and L. Ries, *The Twenty-two Immutable Laws of Branding* (New York: HarperBusiness, 1998).

12. "The Field Service Optimization Benchmark Report," The Aberdeen Group, June 2004.

13. M. A. Cohen, N. Agrawal, and V. Agrawal, "Winning in the Aftermarket," *Harvard Business Review* (May 2006).

14. J. B. Pine II, D. Peppers, and M. Rogers, "Do You Want to Keep Your Customers Forever?," *Harvard Business Review* (March–April 1995): 103–115.

15. Brynjolfsson and Smith, "Frictionless Commerce?"

16. C. Meyer and A. Schwager, "Understanding Customer Experience," *Harvard Business Review* (February 2007).

17. H. Green, "How Amazon Aims to Keep You Clicking," *Business Week,* February 19, 2009.

3

Matching Products, Markets, and Strategies

In the previous chapter, *customer value* is defined as the way that customers view the company's offerings—from product innovation through price all the way to experience and relationships. I argued that different customer value propositions require different operations and supply chain strategies.

This chapter focuses on the effects of customer value, product characteristics, and the sales channel on operations and supply chain strategies. I consider various supply chain strategies including push, pull, and a relatively new paradigm, the push-pull strategy, and develop a framework for matching products and industries with supply chain strategies. Importantly, these concepts and framework provide a deep insight into the appropriate manufacturing strategy that the firm should apply, and this strategy is directly related to the degree of operational flexibility and the sales channel.

Beyond specific frameworks and strategies, two important themes run throughout the chapter. First, customer value, product and channel characteristics significantly affect operations and supply chain strategies. Thus, when the same product is offered through multiple channels (say, retail and online), different supply chain strategies may apply. Second, different portions of the supply chain may require different strategies, and identifying the appropriate one requires a holistic, global view of the entire chain.

3.1   Push, Pull, and Push-Pull Strategies

Traditional supply chain strategies are often categorized as either push or pull strategies. This distinction probably stems from the manufacturing revolution of the 1980s, in which manufacturing systems were divided into these categories. Interestingly, in the last few years, a number of companies have employed a hybrid approach—the push-pull supply chain paradigm.

The Push-Based Supply Chain

In a *push-based supply chain*, production and distribution decisions are based on long-term forecasts. Typically, the manufacturer bases its demand forecasts on orders received from the retailer's warehouses. A push-based supply chain therefore is slow to react to the changing marketplace, which can lead to

· An inability to meet changing demand patterns, and
· The obsolescence of supply chain inventory as demand for certain products disappears.

In addition, variability of orders received from retailers is typically much higher than variability in customer demand, and this increase in variability propagates upstream in the supply chain. This is the so-called bullwhip effect (see appendix A). This increase in variability leads to

· Excessive inventories due to the need for large safety stocks,
· Larger and more variable production batches,
· Unacceptable service levels, and
· Product obsolescence.

Specifically, the bullwhip effect leads to inefficient resource utilization because planning and managing are difficult. For instance, it is not clear how a manufacturer should determine production capacity. Should it be based on peak demand, which implies that most of the time the manufacturer has expensive resources sitting idle, or should it be based on average demand, which requires extra—and expensive—capacity during periods of peak demand? Similarly, it is not clear how to plan transportation capacity—based on peak demand or average demand. Thus, in a push-based supply chain, we often find increased transportation costs, high inventory levels, and high manufacturing costs, due to the need for emergency production changeovers.

The Pull-Based Supply Chain

In a *pull-based supply chain*, production and distribution are demand driven so that they are coordinated with true customer demand rather than forecast demand. In a pure pull system, the firm does not hold any inventory and responds only to specific orders. This is enabled by fast information-flow mechanisms that transfer information about customer demand, e.g., point-of-sale (POS) data, to the various supply chain participants. Pull systems are intuitively attractive since they lead to

· Decreased lead times, which are achieved by better anticipating incoming orders from the retailers,
· Decreased inventory at retailers' warehouses since inventory levels at these facilities increase with lead times,
· Decreased variability in the system and, in particular, variability faced by manufacturers due to lead time reduction, and
· Decreased inventory at the manufacturer due to the reduction in variability.

The following example illustrates the impact of a pull-based supply chain strategy:

Example 3.1

A major apparel manufacturer recently changed its supply chain strategy to a pull-based system. Retailers order from this manufacturer about once a month but transfer POS data much more frequently, usually daily or weekly, which allows the manufacturer to adjust production quantities continuously according to true customer demand.

Thus, in a pull-based supply chain, we typically see a significant reduction in system inventory level, an enhanced ability to manage resources, and a reduction in system costs when compared with the equivalent push-based system.

On the other hand, pull-based systems are often difficult to implement when lead times are so long that it is impractical to react to demand information. Also, in pull-based systems, it is frequently more difficult to take advantage of economies of scale in manufacturing and transportation since planning is not done far ahead to take advantage of this capability.

These advantages and disadvantages of push and pull supply chains have led companies to look for a new supply chain strategy that takes advantage of the best of both. Frequently, this is a push-pull supply chain strategy.

The Push-Pull Supply Chain
In a *push-pull strategy*, some stages of the supply chain, typically the initial stages, are operated in a push-based manner while the remaining stages employ a pull-based strategy. The interface between the

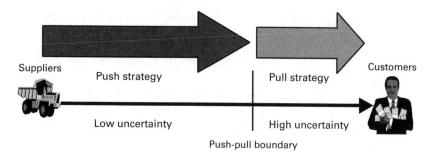

Figure 3.1
The push-pull supply chain time line

push-based stages and the pull-based stages is known as the *push-pull boundary*.

Consider the *supply chain time line*—the time that elapses between procurement of raw material (the beginning of the time line) and the delivery of an order to the customer (the end of the time line). The push-pull boundary is located somewhere along the time line and indicates the point in time when the firm switches from managing the supply chain using one strategy (typically a push strategy) to managing it using a different strategy (typically a pull strategy). This is illustrated in figure 3.1.

Consider a PC manufacturer that builds to stock and thus makes all production and distribution decisions based on forecast. This is a typical push system. By contrast, an example of a push-pull strategy is one in which the manufacturer assembles-to-order. This implies that components inventory are managed based on forecast but that final assembly is in response to a specific customer request. Thus, the push portion of the manufacturer's supply chain is that portion prior to assembly, while the pull part of the supply chain starts with assembly and is performed based on realized customer demand. The push-pull boundary is at the beginning of assembly.

Observe that in this case, the manufacturer takes advantage of *risk pooling*, a strategy driven by following statistical principle:

Rule 3.1   *Aggregate forecasts are always more accurate than individual forecasts.*

Indeed, predicting demand for an individual product is much more difficult than predicting total demand for all products within one product family. Similarly, sales-region forecasts are typically more accurate than sales forecast from an individual store in that region.

By the same token, demand for a component is an aggregation of demand for all finished products that use this component. Since aggregate forecasts are more accurate, uncertainty in component demand is much smaller than uncertainty in finished goods demand, and this leads to safety stock reduction. Dell Computers has used this strategy effectively in its direct-business model and is an excellent example of the impact of the push-pull strategy on supply chain performance.

Postponement or delayed differentiation in product design is also an excellent example of a push-pull strategy. In postponement, the firm designs the product and the manufacturing process so that decisions about which specific product should be manufactured can be delayed as long as possible. The manufacturing process starts by producing a generic or family product, which is differentiated to a specific end product when demand is revealed. The portion of the supply chain prior to product differentiation is typically operated using a push-based strategy. In other words, the generic product is built and transported based on a long-term (aggregate) forecast. Since demand for the generic product is an aggregation of demand for all its corresponding end products, forecasts are more accurate, and inventory levels are reduced. In contrast, customer demand for a specific end product typically has a high level of uncertainty, and product differentiation occurs only in response to individual demand. Thus, the portion of the supply chain starting from the time of differentiation is pull-based.

3.2 Identifying the Appropriate Supply Chain Strategy

What is the appropriate supply chain strategy for a particular product? Should the firm use a push-based supply chain strategy, a pull-based strategy, or a push-pull strategy? Figure 3.2 provides a framework for matching supply chain strategies with products and industries. The vertical axis provides information on uncertainty in customer demand, while the horizontal axis represents the importance of economies of scale, either in production or distribution.

Everything else being equal, higher demand uncertainty leads to a preference for managing the supply chain based on realized demand—a pull strategy. Alternatively, smaller demand uncertainty leads to an interest in managing the supply chain based on a long-term forecast—a push strategy.

Aggregate Planning.
- Push
- economits of sale ind.

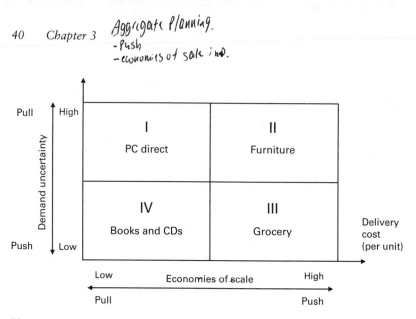

Figure 3.2
Matching supply chain strategies with products: The effect of demand uncertainty and economies of scale

Similarly, everything else being equal, the higher the importance of economies of scale in reducing cost, the greater the value of aggregating demand and thus the greater the importance of managing the supply chain based on long-term forecast—a push-based strategy. If economies of scale are not important, then aggregation does not reduce cost, so a pull-based strategy makes more sense.

In figure 3.2, the area spanned by these two dimensions is divided into four boxes. Box I represents products that are characterized by high uncertainty and by situations in which economies of scale in production, assembly, or distribution are not important. Our framework suggests that a pull-based supply chain strategy is appropriate for these industries and products. This is exactly the direct business strategy that Dell Inc. employs when it allows customers to configure their PCs online and then assembles the product based on individual orders. Because the number of configurations that a customer can choose from is high and since there are no economies of scale in assembly, a high degree of pull is appropriate, which is precisely Dell's strategy.

Box III represents products that are characterized by low demand uncertainty and high economies of scale. Products in the grocery industry such as beer, pasta, and soup belong to that category. Demand for these products is quite predictable, and reducing transportation costs by shipping full truckloads is critical for controlling supply chain costs. In this case, a pull strategy is not appropriate. Indeed, a traditional, push-based retail strategy is appropriate because managing inventory based on long-term forecasts does not increase inventory holding costs while delivery costs are reduced by leveraging economies of scale.

Boxes I and III represent situations in which it is relatively easy to identify an efficient supply chain strategy. In the remaining two cases, there is a mismatch between the strategies suggested by the two attributes—uncertainty and the importance of economies of scale. In these boxes, uncertainty "pulls" the supply chain toward one strategy, while economies of scale "push" the supply chain in a different direction.

For instance, box IV represents products characterized by low demand uncertainty, indicating a push-based supply chain, and low economies of scale, suggesting a pull-based supply chain strategy. Many high-volume, fast-moving books and CDs fall in this category. In this case, a more careful analysis is required, since both traditional retail push strategies and more innovative push-pull strategies may be appropriate, depending on specific costs and uncertainties.

Finally, box II represents products and industries for which uncertainty in demand is high while economies of scale are important in reducing production and delivery costs. The furniture industry is an excellent example of this situation. A typical furniture retailer offers a large number of similar products distinguished by shape, color, fabric, and so forth, and as a result demand uncertainty is high. Because these are bulky products, delivery costs are also high.

In this case, there is a need to distinguish between production and distribution strategies. The production strategy has to follow a pull-based strategy since it is impossible to make production decisions based on long-term forecasts. By contrast, the distribution strategy needs to take advantage of economies of scale to reduce transportation costs. This is exactly the strategy employed by many retailers that do not keep any inventory of furniture. When a customer places an order, the retailer sends it to the manufacturer, which orders the fabric and produces to the customer's specifications. After the product is ready, it is shipped (typically by truck) with many other products to the retail store and from there to the customer. For this purpose, the manufacturer typically has a fixed delivery schedule, and this is used to aggregate all products that are delivered to stores in the same region, thus reducing transportation costs due to economies of scale. Hence, the supply chain strategy followed by furniture manufacturers is, in some sense, a pull-push strategy—production is done based on realized demand, a pull strategy, and delivery is according to a fixed schedule, a push strategy.

Rule 3.2   *The appropriate supply chain strategy—push, pull, or push-pull—is driven by demand uncertainty and economies of scale.*

This powerful rule has been applied by many firms to match product characteristics and supply chain strategies. The same rule is applicable when considering the sales channel. Consider products such as personal computers that can be sold either online or retail. Demand uncertainty and forecast accuracy are quite different in the two channels (see table 2.2). This is true since a typical manufacturer of PCs offers a large variety of configurations online and consequently demand uncertainty is high. By contrast, the same manufacturer typically offers a limited number of configurations through retail store so forecast accuracy is higher. Similarly, because of the volume committed by retailers before the selling season, the retail channel can take advantage of economies of scale, a dimension that is difficult to exploit online. Thus, the retail channel is typically associated with box III and hence a push strategy while the online channel is associated with box I and therefore a high degree of pull.

3.3   Implementing a Push-Pull Strategy

The framework developed in the previous section attempts to characterize the appropriate level of pull and push for different products. For instance, a high degree of pull is appropriate for products that belong to box I in figure 3.2. But achieving the design of the pull system depends on many factors, including product complexity, manufacturing lead times, and supplier and manufacturer relationships. Similarly, there are many ways to implement a push-pull strategy, depending on the location of the push-pull boundary. For instance, Dell locates the push-pull boundary at the assembly point, while furniture manufacturers locate the boundary at the production point.

The discussion so far suggests that the push strategy is applied to the portion of the supply chain where demand uncertainty is relatively small, which makes managing this portion based on long-term forecast appropriate. The pull strategy is applied to the portion of the supply chain time line where uncertainty is high, which makes managing this portion based on realized demand appropriate. This distinction between the two

Table 3.1
Characteristics of the push and pull portions of the supply chain

Portion	Push	Pull
Objective	Minimize cost.	Maximize service level.
Complexity	High	Low
Focus	Resource allocation	Responsiveness
Lead time	Long	Short
Processes	Supply chain planning	Order fulfillment

portions of the supply chain has an important effect on the objectives of the supply chain strategy and on the organizational skills required to manage the system effectively.

Since uncertainty in the push portion of the supply chain is relatively small, service level is not an issue, so the focus can be on *cost minimization*. In addition, this portion of the supply chain is characterized not only by low demand uncertainty and high economies of scale in production and transportation, but and also by long lead times and complex supply chain structures, including product assembly at various levels. Thus, cost minimization is achieved by better utilizing resources such as production and distribution capacities while minimizing inventory, transportation, and production costs.

The pull portion of the supply chain is characterized by high uncertainty, simple supply chain structure, and a short cycle time. Hence, the focus here is on service level which is achieved by deploying a *flexible* and *responsive* supply chain, that is a supply chain that can adapt and respond quickly to changes in customer demand.

This implies that different processes need to be used in different portions of the supply chain. Since the focus in the pull part of the supply chain is on service level, *order-fulfillment processes* are typically applied. Similarly, since the focus of the push part of the supply chain is on cost and resource utilization, supply chain *planning processes* are used to develop an effective strategy for the next few weeks or months. Table 3.1 summarizes the characteristics of the push and pull portions of the supply chain.

Example 3.2

Consider a supplier of fashion skiwear such as Sport Obermeyer.[1] *Every year, the company introduces many new designs or products for which forecast demand is highly uncertain. One strategy used successfully by*

Example 3.2
(continued)

Sport Obermeyer involves distinguishing between high-risk and low-risk designs. Low-risk products (those for which uncertainty and price are low) are produced in advance using long-term forecasts and focusing on cost minimization—a push-based strategy. But decisions on production quantities for high-risk products are delayed until there is a clear market signal on customer demand for each style—a pull strategy. Since fabric lead times are long, the manufacturer typically orders fabric for high-risk products based only on long-term forecasts, well in advance of receiving information about market demand. In this case, the manufacturer takes advantage of the same principle, Rule 3.1, that Dell applies—that aggregate forecasts are more accurate. Since demand for fabrics is an aggregation of demand for all products that use that fabric, demand uncertainty is low, and thus fabric inventory is managed based on a push strategy. So Sport Obermayer uses a push-pull strategy for its high-risk products and a push strategy for its low-risk products.

Notice that the push portion and the pull portion of the supply chain interact only at the push-pull boundary. This is the point along the supply chain time line where there is a need to coordinate the two supply chain strategies, typically through *buffer inventory*. However, this inventory plays a different role in each portion. In the push portion, buffer inventory at the boundary is part of the output generated by the tactical planning process, while in the pull part it represents the input to the fulfillment process.

Thus, the interface between the push portion of the supply chain and the pull portion of the supply chain is forecast demand. This forecast, which is based on historical data obtained from the pull portion, is used to drive the supply chain planning process and determines the buffer inventory.

3.4   The Effect of Lead Time

Undoubtedly, shortening lead time will improve supply chain performance. Indeed, shortening lead times improves the ability to forecast, decreases variability, and hence reduces inventory. So this is an important priority for any organization.

Assuming that lead times cannot be further shortened, the next step is to make sure that the supply chain strategy matches with lead time

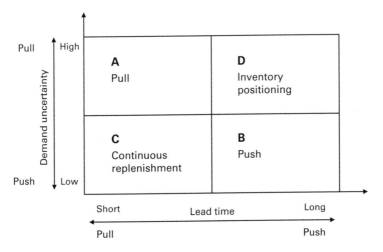

Figure 3.3
Matching supply chain strategies with products: The effect of lead time and demand uncertainty

characteristics. Intuitively, the longer the lead time, the more important it is to implement a push-based strategy. Indeed, it is typically difficult to implement a pull strategy when lead times are so long that it is hard to react to demand information.

In figure 3.3, the effect of lead time and demand uncertainty on supply chain strategy is diagrammed. Box A represents products with short lead times and high demand uncertainty, suggesting that a pull strategy should be applied as much as possible. Again, the PC direct business model is a good example of these types of products and the application of a high degree of pull. Box B represents items with a long supply lead time and low demand uncertainty. Examples include many items in the grocery industry. Again, in this case, the appropriate supply chain strategy is push.

The situation is more challenging for products with the characteristics of boxes C and D. For instance, box C includes products with short supply lead times and highly predictable demand. Good examples are products in the grocery industry with a short life cycle such as bread and dairy products. The retail industry takes advantage of short lead times and low demand uncertainty for these products by using a strategy referred to as *continuous replenishment*. In this strategy, suppliers receive point-of-sale (POS) data and use these data to prepare shipments at previously agreed-on intervals to maintain specific levels of inventory.

Thus, since customer demand drives production and distribution decisions in this supply chain, this strategy is a pull strategy at the production and distribution stages and push at the retail outlets.

Finally, the most difficult supply chains to manage are those associated with box D, where lead times are long and demand is not predictable. Inventory is critical in this type of environment, which requires positioning inventory strategically in the supply chain. Different stages of the supply chain are managed in different ways, depending, among other things, on economies of scale. The stages that keep inventory are managed based on push, and others are managed based on pull. As is shown in the next example, sometimes the entire supply chain is managed based on push.

Example 3.3

A large manufacturer of metal components has a manufacturing facility in China, a central distribution center in China, and many regional and country warehouses serving different markets. Customers include automotive manufacturing companies such as GM, Ford, Toyota, and others. The commitment the manufacturer makes to the original equipment manufacturer (OEM) is that any order will be released from the closest warehouse in less than eight days. Important characteristics of this supply chain include the following:

• The same component is used across multiple assemblies, and
• Lead times for raw material and finished goods (from the China distribution center to the regional and country warehouses) are long.

Recently, the firm has realized that its supply chain is not effective, with too much inventory and at the same time low service levels. A careful examination of the current supply chain strategy used by the firm suggests that inventory is managed using local optimization. Each facility stocks up inventory with little regard for the effect of its decision on supply chain performance. The result of this strategy is a supply chain with a low inventory turnover ratio of about 3.0.

To overcome these challenges, the manufacturer decided to change the way that it positions inventory in the supply chain. The results of this process are described in figure 3.4, which shows both the baseline and the supply chain after the change. Each pie represents inventory at a different location, where light gray is associated with cycle stock and dark gray with safety stock. Most of the safety stock in the optimized supply chain is positioned as plant raw material and at the regional

Example 3.3
(continued)

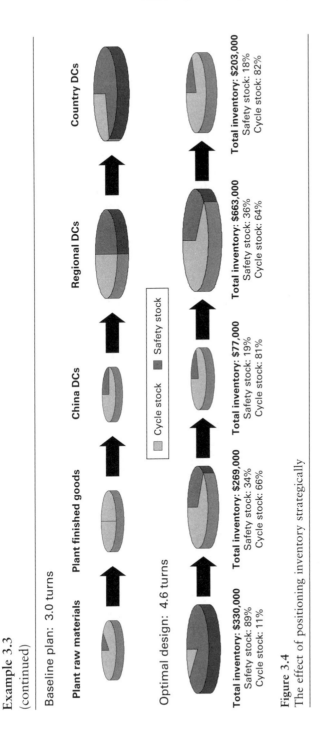

Figure 3.4
The effect of positioning inventory strategically

Example 3.3
(continued)

distribution centers (DCs). In both cases, the reason is risk pooling. Indeed, raw material inventory takes advantage of the risk pooling concepts by aggregating demand across all finished products that use the same component. The regional DCs take advantage of the risk pooling concept by aggregating demand across many country DCs. The net effect of correctly positioning inventory in this supply chain was a significant inventory reduction and an increase to 4.6 turns a year.

Rule 3.3   *Lead times are drivers of the appropriate supply chain strategy.*

3.5   Strategies for Innovative and Functional Products

We now have all the ingredients required to identify the appropriate supply chain strategy for functional and innovative products. Consider again table 2.1 in the previous chapter, where functional products are associated with slow product innovation speed, predictable demand, and low profit margins. Examples include diapers, soup, milk, and tires. On the other hand, innovative products—such as fashion items, cosmetics, or high-tech products—are associated with fast product-innovation speed, unpredictable demand, and high profit margins.

The different characteristics of innovative and functional products imply that the supply chain strategies for innovative products and functional products are very different. It is clear that the appropriate supply chain strategy for functional products is push, where the focus is on efficiency, cost reduction, and supply chain planning. By contrast, the appropriate supply chain strategy for innovative products is pull because of high profit margins, fast technology clock speed, and unpredictable demand. Indeed, here the focus is on responsiveness—time, service level, and order fulfillment. These insights are summarized in figure 3.5.[2]

3.6   Sales Channels, Flexibility, and Manufacturing Strategies

The concepts and framework introduced so far can be used to characterize the appropriate manufacturing strategy that a firm should apply. This strategy depends on the sales channel, the response time that the business

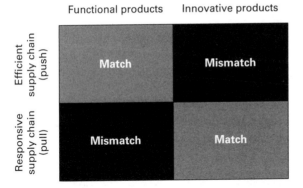

Figure 3.5
Matching product characteristics with strategies. From M. L. Fisher, "What Is the Right Supply Chain for Your Product?," *Harvard Business Review* (March–April 1997): 105–117.

commits to with its customers, and the degree of operational flexibility.

Three manufacturing strategies need to be considered:

• In a build-to-stock strategy, inventory is built based on forecast—a push strategy,
• In an assemble-to-order strategy, individual products are assembled based on customer configuration—a pull strategy, and
• In a build-to-order strategy, lot sizes are produced after receiving a customer order—a pull strategy.

Thus, in a build-to-stock strategy, production is completed typically before customer orders are realized, and in assemble-to-order and build-to-order strategies, production happens after the customer order is received. One way to distinguish between the two is that an assemble-to-order is similar to a build-to-order strategy except that it has a lot size of one and so does not benefit from economies of scale. Build-to-order, on the other hand, takes advantage of economies of scale by "building" lot sizes.

One industry that illustrates this difference between assemble-to-order and build-to-order strategies is the PC industry. Dell sells PCs direct, and its traditional business model is designed around an assemble-to-order strategy where an individual customer order is configured by the assembly line after the order is received. HP's strategy of selling through retailers such as Best Buy implies that the retailer and the manufacturer

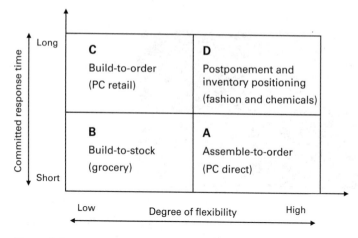

Figure 3.6
Flexibility and the manufacturing strategy

agree on order specifics (such as lot size and configuration) well in advance of the sales period, which allows the manufacturer to produce a large lot based on the retailer requirement—a build-to-order strategy.

Figure 3.6 characterizes the relationships between the committed response time to the customers, the manufacturing strategy, and the firm's degree of flexibility. For example, when the degree of flexibility is high and the committed response time is short (box A), an assemble-to-order strategy is appropriate. This is consistent with the view that in industries where the business sells direct (like the PC industry), a high degree of responsiveness and flexibility is important.

On the other hand, when the degree of flexibility is low and committed response time is short (box B), a build-to-stock strategy—a push strategy—is appropriate. Unlike in PC direct, here the focus is on cost reduction and effective forecast, perhaps using point-of-sales data, much like in the retail business for grocery, soap, diapers, or soft drinks.

For the same degree of flexibility but when committed response time is long—for example, selling high-tech products such as PCs, cell phones, or printers through retailers—a build-to-order strategy is effective (box C). Here, the manufacturer focuses on efficiency or cost reduction, which is achieved through economies of scale in manufacturing and distribution.

Observe an important implication of this framework:

Rule 3.4 *The sales channel determines the manufacturing and distribution strategies.*

To illustrate this rule, recall the analysis in chapter 2, particularly section 2.2, which discusses the challenges and opportunities of selling either online or in traditional retail stores (see table 2.2). The analysis in the current section supports the observation made in that section: selling online implies a large number of possible product configurations (Dell direct) and hence assemble-to-order. By contrast, selling through brick-and-mortar outlets limits the set of choices offered to consumers and hence build-to-order strategies are effective when lead times are long (HP), and build-to-stock strategies are effective when lead times are short (grocery products).

Finally, box D represents industries such as fashion or chemicals that are characterized by a high degree of uncertainty. In the fashion industry, uncertainty is due to the short product life cycle and the fierce market competition. In the chemicals and pharmaceutical industries, this is due to competition and new product introduction.

Two forces affect these industries. On the one hand, manufacturing time is long. In the chemical industry, manufacturing can take more than six months. On the other hand, commitments to customers are long but typically not enough to allow production to start after receiving customer orders. Thus, positioning work-in-process inventory in some manufacturing stages is common in the chemical and pharmaceutical industries. In fashion, postponement and standard parts—such as zippers or fabrics—are typically applied.

3.7 Summary

Many companies have improved their performance by reducing costs, increasing service levels, reducing the bullwhip effect, and improving responsiveness to changes in the marketplace. In many cases, these improvements were facilitated by the implementation of a push, pull, or hybrid push-pull strategy, depending on product characteristics such as product and technology-innovation speed, economies of scale, lead time, and demand uncertainty.

Some of these characteristics are directly related to the value proposition provided by the firm. For example, when selling PCs direct, Dell focuses on customer experience and allows a large variety of product configurations. This increases the level of demand uncertainty and the need for a higher degree of pull.

By contrast, HP sells through retailers and provides a smaller number of configurations hence reducing demand uncertainty and competing on price. Thus, the need for a cost-focused strategy that takes advantage of the ability to forecast accurately—a push-based strategy.

The same is true in the furniture industry. High-end furniture manufacturers offer a large number of similar products that are distinguished by shape, color, fabric, and so forth, and as a result demand uncertainty is very high. Because these are bulky products, delivery costs are also high. These two characteristics drive the need for a pull-push strategy where manufacturing is decoupled from distribution. In this case, production starts after receiving an order (a pull strategy), while distribution is done based on a fixed schedule (a push strategy). This is quite different than the strategy employed by IKEA, a furniture retailer that competes on price and store availability. IKEA offers a small number of stock-keeping units (SKUs) to customers, so it can forecast demand effectively (a push strategy).

This chapter will be incomplete if we do not mention an important function that contributes to operations strategy—the procurement function. The next chapter examines procurement strategies and supply contracts and ways that they can be aligned with and in support of the business strategy.

Acknowledgment

Section 3.5 is in part motivated by Fisher.[3]

Notes

1. M. L. Fisher, J. Hammond, W. Obermeyer, and A. Raman, "Making Supply Meet Demand in an Uncertain World," *Harvard Business Review* (May–June 1994): 83–93.

2. M. L. Fisher, "What Is the Right Supply Chain for Your Product?," *Harvard Business Review* (March–April 1997): 105–117.

3. Ibid.

4

Procurement and Supply Contracts as Competitive Weapons

Until recently, procurement was considered a clerical function that added very little value to the organization. It sat low in the organizational structure and received little attention from senior management. As a result, the best and the brightest were not attracted to this functional area.

Today, procurement is used as a competitive weapon that distinguishes highly profitable companies from others within the same industry. Indeed, a survey of electronics companies identified 19 percent gaps in profitability between the least and the most successful companies, a full 13 percent of which was accounted for by the lower cost of goods sold. In the electronics industry, 60 to 70 percent of the cost of goods sold is attributed to the cost of purchased goods and services.[1]

To show how procurement affects business performance, this chapter reviews the net profit margins of three companies in different industries. In 2008, Pfizer's profit margin was about 16.32 percent compared to Dell's 5.69 percent and Boeing's 3.6 percent. For each company, reducing procurement costs by exactly one percentage point would have translated directly into net profit. To achieve the same effect on net profit through higher sales, Pfizer would need to increase its revenue by 6.13 (0.01 / 0.16) percent, Dell by 17 percent, and Boeing by 27.8 percent. The implications are clear: the smaller the profit margins, the more important it is to reduce procurement costs.

This is well understood by senior management. What is less clear is why recent surveys[2] have found a gap between management objectives—procuring high-quality products at the lowest possible total cost of ownership—and reality—paying higher costs for procurement than expected, earning lower procurement savings than anticipated, and having an acknowledged inefficient procurement organization.

The reason for this gap lies in the origin of the procurement function. For many years, procurement was regarded as a back-office operation focusing almost exclusively on unit cost and applying the same strategy across all or almost all procured products. This approach created barriers between procurement and other business functions—such as product design, manufacturing, and supply chain—and led to misalignment with the firm's customer value proposition. So long as companies were doing well and profit margins were high, no one paid much attention to the procurement function.

As competition has intensified and demand uncertainty and market risks have increased, the procurement function has evolved and for some companies has become "a strategic, proactive process that contributes as much as—or more than—other business functions to profitability."[3] So what are the characteristics of effective procurement processes? What is the link between the firm's customer value proposition and the procurement strategy? How do market and demand risks affect procurement and supply contracts? And finally, what risk-mitigation strategies must procurement follow to deal with (commodity) price or supply risks? These are the topics discussed in this chapter.

4.1 Drivers of Procurement Strategies

Many industries have changed their supply strategies and supplier footprint in the last three decades. In the 1980s, American automotive manufacturing companies focused on suppliers either in the United States or in Germany. This changed in the 1990s, with a shift to suppliers in Mexico, Spain, and Portugal. Finally, in the last few years, these original equipment manufacturers (OEMs) have again changed their supplier footprint with a significant move to China. Similar trends have been observed in the high-tech industry. In the 1980s, U.S. high-tech companies focused on sourcing in the United States; in the 1990s, on Singapore and Malaysia; and recently, on Taiwan and mainland China. These trends are driven by intensified competition, a continuous search for low-cost suppliers, and the fall of market barriers.

These trends do not imply that the same procurement strategy should be applied across all products. On the contrary! The appropriate procurement strategy depends, in part, on the type of products the firm is purchasing and the levels of risk and uncertainty involved. In the automotive industry, for example, the procurement strategy that should be applied to vehicle electronic systems is different than the one applied to transmission systems or to tooling equipment and machines. These items have different characteristics, including level of risk, profit impact, price, technology knowledge, available capacity, initial investment required, and logistics challenges.

This section introduces a framework that can help organizations determine an appropriate procurement strategy and emphasizes the associated capabilities required for a successful implementation. Whatever the procurement strategy, it must integrate with the firm's operations and align with its value proposition. Intuitively, the strategy should depend on factors such as type of product or component purchased, ability to forecast, effect on profit, and technology and product innovation speed.

By now the reader has grasped on the link between a customer value proposition and operations or supply chain strategies. This link suggests that innovative products and functional products need quite different supply chain strategies. Following the discussion in chapter 3, the appropriate supply chain strategy for functional products is push, where the focus is on efficiency, cost reduction, and supply chain planning. Conversely, the appropriate supply chain strategy for innovative products is pull because of high profit margins, fast innovation speed, and unpredictable demand. In this case, the focus is on responsiveness, service level, and order fulfillment (see chapter 3 and table 3.1).

A similar link exists between the customer value proposition and procurement. When a retailer procures functional products, the focus should be on *minimizing total landed cost*—the total cost of purchasing and delivering the product to its final destination. This cost includes

- Unit cost,
- Transportation cost,
- Inventory holding cost,
- Handling cost,
- Duties and taxation, and
- Cost of financing.

When procuring innovative products, however, a focus on total landed cost is not appropriate. Because of the fast innovation speed, high margins, and high forecast error, the objective in this case is on *reducing lead times and improving supply chain responsiveness*.

Thus, when a retailer or a distributor procures functional products, sourcing from low-cost countries (such as mainland China and Taiwan) is appropriate. However, when sourcing innovative products, the focus is on suppliers close to the market demand (where the products are sold). Alternatively, short lead times may be achieved using air shipments, and in this case the trade-off is unit cost versus transportation cost.

The approach discussed here can be extended in a number of directions. For example, consider a brick-and-mortar retailer like Best Buy, which may procure PCs from Hewlett-Packard (HP). The discussion in chapter 2 suggests that the retail channel possesses a number of unique characteristics—low product variety, high forecast accuracy, and high volume. *These characteristics motivate HP to source PCs from low-cost countries and ship the products by sea to reduce total landed costs.*

The underlying assumption in this strategy—that shipping by sea is more cost effective than shipping by air—can be quantified and validated for individual products. This is often true in retail for high-volume, high-forecast-accuracy products. Evidently, shipping by sea takes a significantly longer time than shipping by air and therefore requires a higher pipeline inventory, but the difference in transportation cost renders shipping by air an unattractive option.

So here is an example illustrating procurement complexity—retail sourcing strategies for innovative products such as PCs resemble sourcing for functional products because of the channel characteristics.

Consider now a PC manufacturer that sells products online. Here the channel characteristics are different—high product variety, poor forecast accuracy, and low volume for each configuration. This is where speed and responsiveness are important, and hence two approaches have been applied: assemble products close to market demand, or assemble in low-cost countries and airship to various markets.

The insights gained so far can be applied in the development of a procurement strategy for any finished product or component. For this purpose, we consider five criteria applied to the procured item:

- Forecast accuracy,
- Supply risk,
- Price risk,
- Innovation speed, and
- Financial impact.

When procuring a component, *forecast accuracy* is not necessarily the same as the finished-product forecast accuracy. For example, if the same component is used in multiple finished goods, the risk pooling concept (see rule 3.1) implies higher forecast accuracy at the component level. Poor forecast accuracy implies inventory risk (when supply is far greater than demand) or shortage risk (when supply is below demand). Therefore, everything else being equal, the higher the forecast error, the more important it is to delay ordering decisions as much as possible, until market signals are available. Thus, the focus is on lead time reduction.

Supply risk is estimated in terms of the supplier's financial stability, likelihood of supply shortage, number of suppliers, substitution opportunities, and product quality. *Price risk* is assessed based on price volatility, which is especially important for commodities, exchange-rate uncertainty, or changes in labor costs.

Item and technology *innovation speed* are important in the development of a viable framework because they affect *obsolescence costs*, which are traditionally defined as the costs associated with the item becoming obsolete. The faster the innovation speed, the higher the obsolescence risks. Thus, everything else being equal, the faster the innovation speed, the more important it is to emphasize lead time reduction in procurement.

Finally, *financial impact* is evaluated based on component cost as a percentage of the cost of the finished product, percentage of total purchased cost, or effect on revenue if supply is disrupted. The last observation is important: *low-cost components can have high financial impact if their shortage shuts down the production line.*

Depending on these criteria, the decision may be to focus the sourcing strategy on minimizing total landed costs, lead time reduction, dual sourcing, or increasing flexibility. For example, when component forecast accuracy is high, supply risk is low, price risk is low, innovation speed is slow, and financial impact is high, then a cost-based sourcing strategy is appropriate. That is, in this case, minimizing total landed cost should be the main focus of the procurement strategy. This typically implies sourcing from low-cost countries, such as Asia-Pacific countries.

By contrast, when forecast accuracy is poor, innovation speed is fast, and financial impact is high, a sourcing strategy based on lead time reduction is appropriate.

If supply and price risks also are high, then dual sourcing, flexibility, and lead time reduction are the focus of the sourcing strategy. It is not clear how a company best achieves all these objectives. One solution is to apply a portfolio approach. This approach combines fixed-quantity contracts (enabling short lead times through carrying inventory), option contracts (flexibility), and spot markets (multiple supply sources), as illustrated in the following example.

Example 4.1

In 2000, Hewlett-Packard was facing an important challenge. Demand for Flash memory was growing so rapidly that Flash memory price and supply were uncertain. Uncertainty in Flash memory price, supply, and

Example 4.1
(continued)

---

demand implied significant financial and supply risks. If HP committed to purchase a large amount of inventory, it could be exposed to a huge financial risk through obsolescence cost. If it did not have enough supply, then the firm would be exposed to both supply risk and financial risk, since purchasing from the spot market during shortage periods would require premium payments. HP's solution was the portfolio strategy, where it combined fixed commitment, option contracts, and spot purchasing.[4]

Figure 4.1 summarizes the framework in more detail. It provides an approach for evaluating component sourcing strategy by integrating the effect of the five drivers. To illustrate the framework, consider the procurement of car seats in the automotive industry. Car seats are typically used in a variety of models, so forecast accuracy is high. There are many suppliers, so supply and price risks are low. The technology does not change frequently. Finally, these are expensive items, so financial impact is high. These characteristics suggest that a procurement strategy should focus on forcing competition among suppliers and minimizing total landed costs.

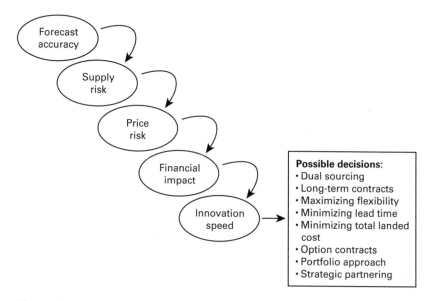

Figure 4.1
A qualitative approach for evaluating component sourcing strategy

A careful review of the framework developed here suggests that procurement must possess capabilities to mitigate, reduce the impact of, or completely eliminate supply and price risks. The next two sections thus examine strategies for reducing exposure to supply and price risks.

4.2   Reducing Exposure to Supply Risk

Supply risk refers to a potential disruption of supply due to a supplier's financial stability, a supply shortage because of a supplier's production or distribution problems, product quality problems, or other sources of less predictable risks such as hurricanes or earthquakes. Three different cases can be distinguished, depending on component price and financial impact (see figure 4.2).

First, when component price is low but financial impact is high—that is, when component shortage will shut down production lines—it is critical to ensure supply. This can be accomplished by investing in inventory or by implementing dual sourcing strategies. Alternatively, flexibility—achieved through system, process, or product design—can deal effectively with supply risks. For example, system flexibility allowed Pepsi Bottling Group to instantaneously respond to a supply disruption caused by fire at a chemical plant near one of its suppliers, see chapter 1. Similarly, product-design flexibility enabled Nokia to recover quickly from a supply disruption caused by fire at a supplier's facility, Philips

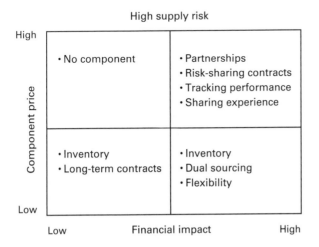

Figure 4.2
Risk-mitigation strategies when supply risk is high

Semiconductor's factory in Albuquerque, New Mexico. Finally, process flexibility allowed Toyota to quickly restart the supply of P-valves after a major disruption (see chapter 5 for both case studies).

Second, consider expensive components with high financial impact and high supply risks, such as car engines and transmission systems. These are the items that strongly affect customer experience, and their price is a large portion of total system cost. These are typically referred to as *strategic* components,[5] and their suppliers are considered *strategic suppliers*.

These components typically have a single supplier.[6] Clearly, the most appropriate supply strategy for these items is to focus on long-term partnerships with suppliers and implement effective supply contracts where risks are shared with suppliers (risk-sharing strategies are discussed in section 4.4). In addition, tracking the operational and financial performance of these suppliers and sharing risk-mitigation strategies and experiences can help anticipate and reduce the likelihood of an unfortunate supply disruption.

Finally, consider components with low financial impact and price. These components do not contribute a large portion of the product cost, but their supply is risky. Because such components typically have few suppliers, these suppliers enjoy a power position.[7] For these items, ensuring continuous supply, even possibly at a premium cost, is important. This can be done through long-term contracts or by carrying stock or both.

4.3   Mitigating Exposure to Price Risk

Mitigating price risks is perhaps one of the most important and difficult challenges faced by the procurement function. Indeed, commodity products such as coffee beans, cotton, grain, milk, oil, computer memory, electricity, rubber, and steel are subject to enormous price volatility. These commodities are available from a large number of suppliers as well as the spot market.

Unfortunately, there are significant downsides to spot trading.[8] First, spot-price volatility is high because supply and sometimes demand for many commodities are highly seasonal. Second, there is a natural spread between the buy and sell prices in these markets. At any given instance, the sell price is lower than the buy price in spot markets, so trading can be costly. Third, not all possible supplies of the same commodity have the same reliability or compatibility with the buyer requirements.[9] This implies that spot purchasing may incur an additional cost that is associated with adaptation and compatibility—a cost that is above and beyond the purchase price. Thus, spot purchasing, a reactive strategy, creates inefficiencies and typically contributes to market-price volatility.

Similarly, long-term contracts, sometimes referred to as *fixed-quantity* or *forward contracts,* are a proactive strategy. They require buyers to predict both demand and commodity prices. But predicting demand may lead to shortages or inventory write-offs. Outguessing commodity prices may lead a buyer to commit to a price that is significantly higher than what its competitors are paying. This is true since predicting commodity prices requires a deep understanding of micro (supply and demand) and macro (weather, geopolitical issues, currency fluctuations) conditions, which are difficult to pinpoint. Hence, long-term fixed-quantity contracts are very risky.

When should the organization rely on spot-market contracts and when on long-term contracts? How can the firm balance spot-market risks and opportunities? And, most important, what can be done to mitigate price risks? These questions are addressed below.

Figure 4.3 illustrates the appropriate mitigation strategies when price risk is high for situations that depend on financial impact and commodity price assessed as a percentage of the entire product cost.

Consider situations where commodity price and financial impact are low. This is the case for consumer packaged goods, particularly in the food

Figure 4.3
Risk-mitigation strategies when price risk is high

and beverage industries, where commodities such as water, corn, and soybeans are used as ingredients. In this case, a common practice is to transfer some of the commodity price increase to the consumer. The low commodity price typically implies a relatively small effect on consumers and hence on market demand. Of course, in an economic recession, firms are reluctant to increase price significantly. Thus, in parallel, negotiating long-term contracts and investing in inventory are also appropriate.

Next, when commodity price is low but financial impact is high, no one wants to rely on the spot market, which may well lead to shortages when there is a limited supply of components. As before, a low component price implies that the focus of the procurement organization should be on inventory, long-term contracts, and the transfer of some of the price increase to consumers. Unfortunately, this is typically not enough. The high financial impact calls for a proactive approach to guarantee supply if demand is higher than expected. Indeed, depending on demand uncertainty, option contracts, sometimes referred to as *flexible-quantity contracts,* may be required to deal with poor forecast accuracy. So what are option contracts?

Option Contracts

One way to reduce the risks associated with uncertain demand is through *option contracts.* In these contracts, the buyer prepays a relatively small fraction of the product price in return for a commitment from the supplier to reserve capacity up to a certain level. The initial payment is typically referred to as *reservation price* or *premium.* If the buyer does not *exercise* the option, the initial payment is lost. The buyer can purchase any amount of supply up to the option level by paying an additional price for each unit that is agreed to at the time the contract is signed. This additional price is referred to as *execution price* or *exercise price.* With this type of contract, the total price—reservation price plus execution price—that the buyer pays for each purchased unit is typically higher than the unit price in a long-term contract.

Because option contracts provide the buyer with flexibility to adjust order quantities depending on realized demand, these contracts reduce the buyer's risks. Thus, these contracts shift risks from the buyer to the supplier since the supplier is now exposed to customer demand uncertainty. This is in contrast to long-term contracts in which the buyer takes all the risk.

Finally, consider the case in figure 4.3, which occurs when both commodity price and financial impact are high. This challenging scenario combines high price risk with the inventory and shortage risks that are associated with demand uncertainly. Inventory risk is an important procurement driver because high commodity prices imply that inventory is expensive. Similarly, shortage risk is a driver since the high financial impact suggests that shortages may have a devastating effect on the bottom line. This is where a few innovative companies have applied portfolio contracts.

Portfolio Contracts

In *portfolio contracts*, buyers sign simultaneously multiple contracts to optimize their expected profits and reduce their risks. The contracts differ in price and level of flexibility, thus allowing the buyer to hedge against inventory, shortage, and spot-price risk. This approach is particularly meaningful for commodity products, since a large pool of suppliers is available, each offering a different type of contract. Thus, the buyer may select several different complementary contracts to manage risks and reduce expected procurement and inventory holding costs.

To find effective portfolio contracts, the buyer needs to identify the appropriate mix of low price and no-flexibility (fixed-quantity) contracts, reasonable price but better flexibility (option) contracts, and unknown price and unknown quantity (spot market). The buyer must optimize between the different contracts—long-term (fixed-quantity) commitment, option level (the amount of capacity to buy from companies selling option contracts), and the level of supply that should be left uncommitted. The following discussion sheds more light on portfolio contracts.

When Victor Martinez-de-Albeniz from IESE Business School in Barcelona, Spain, and I conducted our research on procurement contracts between 2001 and 2003, we were struck by the similarities that we saw between the challenges faced by procurement officers and those of financial investors. Much like financial investments, procurement can choose between different contracts (or securities, in the case of financial investments) that are characterized by cost (or return) and risk. The higher (or lower) the cost (or return), the lower the procurement (or investment) risk. The procurement objective, much like the objective of a financial investor, is to find the right trade-off between cost and risk exposure. In that respect, portfolio contracts—similar to investment portfolios—are driven by a set of market scenarios that collectively represent the demand forecast.

Consider a demand forecast that includes three scenarios—low demand (the worst case), high demand (the best case), and medium demand (an intermediate case). A portfolio contract thus will invest in long-term, fixed-quantity contracts at the low demand level since demand is "guaranteed" not to fall below that level. It will purchase option contracts from one or more suppliers for an amount equal to the difference between the medium and low demand levels, since this part of the demand is uncertain, but the level of uncertainty is not high. Finally, it will leave as uncommitted any demand above the medium level and rely on spot markets because of the high uncertainty associated with the best-case scenario.[10]

An example of the portfolio approach is HP's strategy for the procurement of electricity or memory products. About 50 percent of HP's procurement cost is invested in long-term contracts, 35 percent in option contracts, and the remaining in the spot market.[11]

An essential component of the portfolio strategy is the ability to trade commodities. Trading, traditionally a responsibility of the chief financial officer, must be aligned with the procurement strategy to provide a comprehensive risk-mitigation strategy. For companies operating in global markets, trading implies coordination with procurement, logistics, and supply chain because operations in one region may have the option to exploit local spot trading (trading in its own market) or the option to utilize capacity available in other regions. Therefore, pooling capacity across existing resources and spot markets, local or global, should be viewed as the best way to match supply and demand in face of price, supply, and demand risks.

One important characteristic that the organization needs when relying on a combination of long-term contracts and spot purchasing is the ability to adapt efficiently to trading with new suppliers. The manufacturer needs to be sufficiently flexible in product substitution—for example, through a process flexibility or modular product-design strategy—so that its reliance on a given supplier is low. It can switch between components from various long-term partners as well as new suppliers found on the spot market with relatively low (or no) value loss.

To summarize, the analysis in sections 4.2 and 4.3 suggests the following:

Rule 4.1   *The higher the supply and price risks, the more important it is to invest in procurement flexibility—the ability to effectively and efficiently switch from one supplier to another.*

4.4   Risk-Sharing Contracts

Effective procurement strategies for strategic components require the development of relationships with suppliers. These relationships can take many forms, both formal and informal, but to ensure adequate supplies and timely deliveries, buyers and suppliers agree on supply contract terms. These contracts address issues that arise between a buyer and a supplier, whether the buyer is a manufacturer purchasing raw materials from a supplier, an original equipment manufacturer purchasing components from a contract manufacturer, or a retailer purchasing goods. As we shall see, supply contracts are powerful tools that can be used for far more than ensuring an adequate supply of goods.

To illustrate the importance and effect of different types of supply contracts on supply chain performance, consider a typical two-stage supply chain consisting of a buyer and a supplier. The sequence of events in such a supply chain is as follows: the buyer generates a forecast, determines how many units to order from the supplier, and places an order to the supplier to optimize its profit, and the supplier reacts to the order placed by the buyer. This process is referred to as a *sequential supply chain* since decisions are made sequentially. In a sequential supply chain, each party determines its own course of action independent of the effect of its decisions on other parties in the supply chain. Undoubtably, this cannot be an effective strategy for supply chain partners since it does not identify what is best for the entire supply chain.

It is natural to look for mechanisms that enable supply chain entities to move beyond this sequential process and toward *global optimization*. To identify mechanisms that allow supply chain parties to improve profit for all parties, we make the following observation. In supply chains such as the one described previously, the buyer assumes all of the risk of having more inventory than sales, while the supplier takes no risk. Since the supplier takes no risk, she would like the buyer to order as much as possible, while the buyer limits his order quantity because of the huge financial risk. Since the buyer limits his order quantity, the likelihood of out of stock is significantly increased.

If the supplier is willing and able to share some of the risk with the buyer, then it may be profitable for the buyer to order more items, thereby reducing the probability of out of stock and increasing profit for both supplier and buyer. It turns out that a variety of supply contracts enable this risk-sharing process and therefore increase profits for both supply chain entities.

Buy-Back Contracts

In *buy-back contracts*, the seller agrees to buy back unsold goods from the buyer for some agreed-on price. This provides the buyer with incentives to order more units since the risk associated with unsold units is reduced. At the same time, the supplier's risk clearly increases. Thus, the contract is designed such that the increase in order quantity placed by the buyer—and hence the decrease in the likelihood of out of stock— more than compensates the supplier for the increase in risk.

Revenue-Sharing Contracts

In a sequential supply chain, the buyer orders a limited number of units because the supplier charges a high purchase price. If somehow the buyer can convince the supplier to reduce the wholesale price, then the buyer will have an incentive to order more units. But a reduction in purchase price will decrease the supplier's profit if it is unable to sell more units. This is addressed by revenue-sharing contracts. In a revenue-sharing contract, the buyer shares some of its revenue with the seller in return for a discount on the purchase price. That is, in this contract, the buyer transfers a portion of the revenue from each unit sold to the end customer.

Global Optimization

The two contracts described above raise an important question: what is the most profit that both supplier and buyer can hope to achieve? To answer this question, we take a different approach. What if an unbiased decision maker is allowed to identify the best strategy for the entire supply chain? This unbiased decision maker would consider the two supply chain partners, the supplier and the buyer, as two members of the same organization. That is, the transfer of money between the parties is ignored, and the unbiased decision maker will maximize supply chain profit, thus achieving *global optimization*.

This kind of unbiased decision maker is rare, but effective supply contracts provide incentives for supply chain partners to replace traditional strategies, in which each partner optimizes its own profit, with global optimization where total supply chain profit is maximized. The difficulty with global optimization is that it requires the firm to surrender decision-making power to an unbiased decision maker. This is precisely why supply contracts are important.

Rule 4.2 *Effective supply contracts help firms achieve global optimization by allowing buyers and suppliers to share risks and potential benefits.*

Indeed, it can be shown that *carefully designed supply contracts achieve the same profit as global optimization.*

From an implementation point of view, the main drawback with global optimization is that it does not provide a mechanism for allocating supply chain profit between the partners. It provides information only on the best, or optimal, set of actions that need to be taken by the supply chain to improve profit. In contrast, supply contracts allocate this profit among supply chain members.

Equally important, effective supply contracts allocate profit to each partner in a way that no partner can improve its profit by deciding to deviate from the optimal set of decisions. That is, there is no incentive for either buyer or seller to deviate from the set of actions that will achieve the global optimal solution.

The following example illustrates the impact of supply contracts in practice.

Example 4.2

Until 1998, video rental stores used to purchase copies of newly released movies from the movie studios for about $65 and rent them to customers for $3. Because of the high purchase price, rental stores did not buy enough copies to cover peak demand, which typically occurs during the first ten weeks after a movie is released on video. The result was a low customer-service level: in a 1998 survey, about 20 percent of customers reported that they could not get their first choice of movie. That year, Blockbuster Video entered into a revenue-sharing contract with the movie studios in which the wholesale price was reduced from $65 to $8 per copy and studios were paid 30 to 45 percent of the rental price of every rental. This revenue-sharing contract had a huge effect on Blockbuster revenue and market share. Today, revenue sharing is used by most large video rental stores.[12]

If these types of supply contracts are so effective, why don't more and more companies apply them in practice? The answer lies in the various implementation drawbacks. First, buy-back contracts require the supplier to have an effective reverse logistics system and indeed may increase its logistics cost. In addition, when retailers sell competing products— some under buy-back contracts while others are not— they have an incentive to push the products that are not under the buy-back contract. This is true, since the retailer's risk is much higher for the products not under the buy-back contract. Therefore, this contract, while intuitively appealing, is used mostly in the book and magazine industries, where retailers do not have an influence on diverting demand from one product to another, and unsold magazines are destroyed by the retailer. Only the first page of the magazine is sent back to the publisher as proof that the product was destroyed.

Revenue-sharing contracts also have limitations. They require the supplier to monitor the buyer's revenue and thus increase administrative costs. The importance of monitoring the revenue is illustrated by the following two litigation stories.

Example 4.3

A lawsuit was brought by three independent video retailers who complained that they had been excluded from receiving the benefits of revenue sharing. Their complaint was dismissed by a judge in June 2002, who stated that the independent retailers did not have the information infrastructure that would have allowed the studios to monitor revenue.

Information technology is not enough. Building trust between the supplier and the buyer is important and yet is difficult to achieve, as is illustrated by the next example.

Example 4.4

In January 2003, the Walt Disney Company sued Blockbuster, accusing the video company of cheating Disney's video unit of approximately $120 million under a four-year revenue-sharing agreement.

Finally, another important limitation is that in revenue sharing, buyers have an incentive to push competing products that have higher profit margins. Revenue-sharing contracts typically reduce the buyer's profit margin since a portion of the revenue is transferred to the supplier. The buyer therefore has an incentive to push other products, particularly similar products from competing suppliers with whom the buyer has no revenue-sharing agreement.

4.5 Supply Contracts between Original Equipment Manufacturers and Contract Manufacturers

A key assumption in all the contracts discussed so far is that the supplier has a make-to-order manufacturing environment. This implies that in the sequential supply chain analyzed earlier, the supplier takes no risk, while the buyer takes all the risk. The contracts described earlier suggest mechanisms for transferring some of the risk from the buyer to the supplier. A relevant question is what the appropriate contracts are when the supplier has a make-to-stock (MTS) supply chain.

This is an important question in today's business environment, since in the last few years, companies have significantly increased the level of outsourcing of everything from the manufacturing of specific components to the design and assembly of the entire product. Consider the following example:

Example 4.5

Ericsson sells telecommunication network equipment to AT&T ,and purchases components from a variety of suppliers, such as Flextronics. Due to significant differences in component lead times, the two companies implement different manufacturing strategies. Flextronics has a make-to-stock environment that is dictated in part by component lead times, while Ericsson makes production decisions only after receiving an order from AT&T. All the risk is taken by Flextronics.

Here, Ericsson (the original equipment manufacturer) assembles products after receiving orders from its customer, AT&T, while Flextronics (the contract manufacturer) produces to stock and needs to build capacity before receiving orders from Ericsson. In this supply chain, the contract manufacturer takes all the risk, while the OEM takes no risk. Because the contract manufacturer assumes all of the risk of building more capacity than sales while the OEM takes no risk, it is not clear that the contract manufacturer will build enough capacity. This is bad practice for both parties. Indeed, since the OEM takes no risk, it would like the contract manufacturer to build as much capacity as possible, while the contract manufacturer limits its production quantity because of the huge financial risk. *limited transparency,*

So, there is clearly an asymmetry in the level of risks faced by each party. Similarly, there may be an asymmetry between the information about market demand available to each party. Consider again the previous example, where Flextronics builds production capacity based on forecasts received from Ericsson, the company that has the relationship with the end customer, AT&T. A forecast received by Flextronics from Ericsson may be inflated, but there is no way to verify it. Indeed, since there is always a positive probability that the forecast is higher than realized demand, the supplier cannot argue that this gap is due to inflated forecasts.

It is not clear that this is a real issue between Ericsson and Flextronics. But the evidence suggests that "forecasts by electronics and telecom companies are often inflated."[14]

So here is one of the most critical challenges typically not well understood by management engaged in outsourcing and contract manufacturing: asymmetry both in the level of risk faced by and the information available to the OEM and the contract manufacturer. Such a discrepancy leads to all sorts of inefficiencies in the supply chain, including supply shortages and higher costs.

How can supply chain partners address this challenge? Observe that in a sequential supply chain, the contract manufacturer often does not produce enough capacity because of high production costs. If somehow the contract manufacturer can convince the OEM to share some of the production costs, then, no doubt, the contract manufacturer will have an incentive to produce more units. But paying part of the production costs will decrease the OEM's profit if it is unable to sell more units. This is addressed through *cost-sharing contracts* where the OEM shares some of the production costs with the manufacturer in return for a discount on the purchase price. *Effectively Sharing the risk.*

Cost-sharing contracts require the contract manufacturer to share its production cost information with the OEM, something contract manufacturers are reluctant to do. So how are these contracts implemented in practice?

The issue often is addressed through an agreement in which the OEM purchases—from the suppliers of the contract manufacturer—one or more components that the contract manufacturer needs. The components remain on the OEM books but are shipped to the contract manufacturer's facility for the production of the finished good. This implies that cost-sharing contracts transfer some risk from the contract manufacturer to the OEM and provide information to the contract manufacturer about the OEM's understanding of market demand—since the supply of parts from the OEM to the contract manufacturer must be aligned with the OEM's market expectations.

Motorola, for example, reported applying this type of contract with its contract manufacturers.[15] Motorola uses its buying power to purchase key components used by the contract manufacturer from the contract manufacturer's suppliers. The components are delivered to the contract manufacturer either in consignment (the OEM still owns the parts at the contract manufacturer) or in a buy-sell engagement (Motorola sells the parts to the contract manufacturer). Motorola's buying power allows it to receive a better price than the contract manufacturer receives from its supplier. Equally important, this strategy guarantees that any competitor of Motorola that buy parts from the same contract manufacturer does not benefit from the Motorola's (the OEM) buying power.

4.6 Summary

Specific frameworks and methods have been applied by innovative companies to transform procurement from a clerical, back-office function into a strategic weapon. Beyond specific techniques, however, there are capabilities that traditional procurement did not possess, including procurement risk management, active commodity trading, pooling capacity across all available resources (including internal capacity), spot trading, risk-sharing strategies, and investing in flexibility—system, process or product-design flexibility—to allow shifting seamlessly between suppliers.

But capabilities are not enough. Management must ensure that the procurement strategy is aligned with and supports the business strategy. Too often, procurement sets its own agenda, not realizing the effect of its decisions on operations and supply chains. In many cases, this is directly related to organizational structure: where procurement sits and how it is viewed by senior management can have a huge effect on business performance.

Lastly, procurement software has added significant value and contributed to the success of many companies by automating the requisition process, allowing visibility for new suppliers, providing information on price and product quality, and allowing online negotiation, contract management, and compliance (see chapter 6 for more on this issue).

But managing price and supply risks are only part of a broader challenge—that of managing risk in the supply chain. Indeed, a failure to manage risk—such as supplier risk—can wipe out an entire organization. The difficulty is that there are many man-made and natural sources of risks: some are controllable, some can be anticipated, and others are rare but have a significant impact. With all these complexities, how can the firm prepare for them? What principles can help companies mitigate these sources of risks? And who in the organization should be responsible for managing risks? These topics are discussed in the next chapter.

Notes

1. J. Kluge, "Reducing the Cost of Goods Sold," *McKinsey Quarterly*, no. 2 (1997): 212–215.
2. "High Performance through Procurement," Accenture (2006), available at http://www.accenture.com (accessed on December 23, 2009); "Global Trade Benchmarks," Aberdeen (2005).
3. "High Performance through Procurement."

4. V. Nagali, J. Hwang, D. Sanghera, M. Gaskins, M. Pridgen, T. Thurston, P. Mackenroth, D. Branvold, P. Scholler, and G. Shoemaker, "Procurement Risk Management (PRM) at Hewlett-Packard Company," *Interfaces* 38, no. 1 (2005): 51–60.

5. P. Kraljic, "Purchasing Must Become Supply Management," *Harvard Business Review* (September–October 1983): 109–117.

6. M. C. J. Caniels and C. J. Gelderman, "Purchasing Strategies in Kraljic Matrix: A Power and Dependence Perspective," *Journal of Purchasing and Supply Management* 11 (2005): 141–155.

7. Ibid.

8. P.-E. Pie, D. Simchi-Levi, and T. I. Tunca, "Sourcing Flexibility, Spot Trading, and Procurement Contract Structure," Working paper, Massachusetts Institute of Technology, Cambridge, Mass., 2009.

9. O. E. Williamson, "The Economics of Organization: The Transaction Cost Approach," *American Journal of Sociology* 87, no. 3 (1981): 548–575; O. E. Williamson, "The Modern Corporation: Origins, Evolution, Attributes," *Journal of Economic Literature* 19, no. 4 (1981): 1537–1568.

10. For detailed analysis, the reader is referred to V. Martinez-de-Albeniz and D. Simchi-Levi, "A Portfolio Approach to Procurement Contracts," *Production and Operations Management* 14, no. 1 (2005): 90–114; V. Martinez de Albeniz and D. Simchi-Levi, "Mean-Variance Trade-offs in Supply Contracts," *Naval Research Logistics* 53, no. 7 (2006): 603–616; and V. Martinez-de-Albeniz and D. Simchi-Levi, "Competition in the Supply Option Market," *Operations Research* 57, no. 5 (2009): 1082–1097.

11. J. Carbone, "HP Buyers Get Hands on Design," 2001, available at http://www.purchasing.com (accessed on December 23, 2009).

12. G. P. Cachon and M. A. Lariviere, "Supply Chain Coordination with Revenue Sharing Contracts: Strengths and Limitations," Working paper, Wharton School, University of Pennsylvania, Philadelphia, 2000.

13. Ö. Özer, "Strategic Commitments for an Optimal Capacity Decision under Symmetric Forecast Information," PowerPoint presentation, 2003; Ö. Özer and W. Wei, "Strategic Commitments for an Optimal Capacity Decision under Asymmetric Forecast Information," *Management Science* 52, no. 8 (2006): 1238–1257.

14. "The Inventory Mess," *Business Week*, March 19, 2001, available at http://www.businessweek.com (accessed on March 24, 2010).

15. Q. Samelson, "Buy/Sell Price-Masking and Outsourcing," Motorola, CSCMP presentation, 2005.

5

Risk Mitigation Strategies

Increasing competition in the manufacturing industry is leading to mounting pressure to reduce supply chain costs. Companies are responding by pursuing strategies such as outsourcing, off-shoring, and lean manufacturing to retain market position or gain competitive advantage. Unfortunately, such cost-cutting measures are sometimes adopted at the expense of managing risk within the supply chain.

Indeed, current industry trends correlate directly to the rising risk levels in the supply chain. As off-shoring and globalization of manufacturing operations continue to grow, supply chains are geographically more diverse and therefore exposed to various types of natural and man-made disasters. Similarly, for lean manufacturers that focus on low inventory levels, one disaster can bring their businesses to a halt.

With the threat of megadisasters an increasing reality, industries need to establish risk mitigation measures that accurately reflect their levels of risk exposure. Unfortunately, while many companies are concerned with supply chain resiliency, only a small fraction of them actively and effectively manage risk.

The increase in the level of risk faced by the enterprise demands that supply chain executives systematically address extreme risks (such as port closings and natural disasters like hurricanes, epidemics, and earthquakes) as well as operational risks (such as forecast errors, sourcing problems, transportation breakdowns, and recall issues). Unfortunately, little can be done after a disaster has occurred. Companies therefore need to plan their supply chains so that they can better respond to both megadisasters and mundane operational problems.

One important human-made risk that has increased in the last few years is associated with fake products and counterfeits. Indeed, globalization has increased the risk that counterfeit and illegitimate prescription medicines will enter the supply chain, which poses health risks to the patients who ingest the medications and leads to loss of revenue for the manufacturer. Similarly, counterfeit computer parts and electronic equipment are responsible for loss of revenue and may imperil product functioning and organizational operations.

This chapter examines various risks that are inherent in global supply chains and techniques that can mitigate these risks.

5.1   Many Sources of Risks

Global supply chains are exposed to some of the same risks that are faced by domestic supply chains and also experience additional risks that are associated with international trade. Figure 5.1 provides a nonexhaustive list of the various types of risks faced by global companies. Natural disasters, geopolitical events, epidemics, and terrorist attacks can shut down production lines because of lack of parts inventory. This happened to some auto manufacturers after the September 11, 2001, terrorist attacks on the United States.

Unfortunately, there is little experience to draw on to prepare for natural megadisasters such as hurricanes Katrina (2005) or Andrew (1992). Similarly, a viral epidemic like the 2003 SARS (severe acute respiratory syndrome) epidemic can shut down the flow of components and products from Asia to the rest of the world but is difficult to prepare

Figure 5.1
Risk sources and their characteristics

for because of lack of data. Following former Secretary of Defense Donald Rumsfeld, we refer to these types of risks as the *unknown-unknowns*: these risks are associated with scenarios where it is difficult to quantify the likelihood of occurrence.

At the other end of the spectrum shown in figure 5.1 are sources of risks such as supplier performance, forecast accuracy, and operational problems. These risks can be quantified and consequently are referred to as *known-unknowns*. For example, using historical data, a firm can characterize forecast error, mean time between machine failure, and supplier lead time performance.

Due to their nature, unknown-unknowns are difficult to control, while known-unknowns are more controllable. Between the two extremes are various types of risks that can be controlled to a certain extent. For example, risks associated with volatile fuel prices can be managed through long-term contracts, while fluctuating exchange rates can be managed through a variety of hedging strategies (discussed below).

Because organizations have different levels of control over the various sources of risks, they need to quantify the expected effects of these risks. *Expected impact* is defined as the product of (1) the likelihood that the risk will materialize and (2) the risk's potential direct effect on business—measured, for instance, by its effect on revenue or profit.

For example, for a company that sources key components from China, political instability in that country could be highly damaging. Because the likelihood of political problems and instability in China is low, the expected impact on the company is medium. By contrast, changes in commodity prices would have a relatively high expected impact. This is true since volatility in commodity prices is high and hence the likelihood of a price change in an unfavorable direction is high. If this happens, the impact on procurement costs can be high. Therefore high expected impact.

The two dimensions—the ability to control each source of risk and its expected impact—motivate the risk assessment framework depicted in figure 5.2. Controllable risk sources with high expected impact can and must be managed effectively. More challenging but equally important is developing risk mitigation strategies for the uncontrollable sources of risks that have high expected impact. Controlled or uncontrolled, management must map out the firm's risk portfolio in a similar fashion to what is done in our risk assessment framework so that gaps and challenges in the company's risk management strategies can be identified.

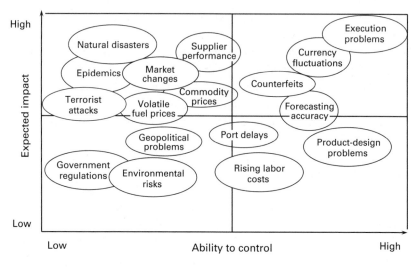

Figure 5.2
The risk assessment framework: Ability to control versus expected impact

A deeper review of the risk assessment framework suggests that management needs to develop risk mitigation strategies that depend on expected impact on business performance. This implies that business objectives and performance need to be matched with risk management strategies. The most effective way to achieve this is to follow this chapter's first rule:

Rule 5.1   *Integrate risks into operational and business decisions.*

Put differently, risk management is not an independent function in the organization but rather must be embedded in the firm's decision-making process. Production sourcing decisions, for example, should take into account at the design stage the expected effect of supply disruption on business performance. This approach calls for an organizational culture that fosters risk assessment and risk management as part of day-to-day decision making.

Example 5.1

CEMEX, one of Mexico's largest companies, specializes in building materials and operates in more than thirty countries. Competing in one of the world's toughest markets, CEMEX faces multiple layers of risks— operational risks (including price and demand risks), market risks

Example 5.1
(continued)

(including market-access and environmental-regulation risks), and global risks (including exchange-rate and energy-price risks). Two themes characterize CEMEX's risk management strategy. First, embracing rather than avoiding specific kinds of risks has become a core competence. For example, the firm pools capacity through spot trading to reduce commodity-price risk and increase value by better matching supply and demand. Second, risk management is so embedded in the company's cultural and organizational fabric that it is barely noticeable as a distinct management function at either the strategic or tactical level. For instance, strategically, the firm integrates risks management in its planning for production capacity and sourcing decisions, and operationally, it reduces risk by actively trading cement across markets. The result is that CEMEX matches or beats global industry standards in managing risks inherent in cement and concrete production and distribution, despite its considerable exposure to multiple layers of risks, especially in emerging markets.[1]

So what methods can a (global) firm apply to mitigate natural and man-made risks? The next two sections consider strategies for dealing with unknown-unknowns (section 5.2) and for dealing with intermediate risks, that is those that are closer to the known-unknown end of the risk spectrum (section 5.3).

5.2   Managing the Unknown-Unknown

[handwritten annotation: risk that is not yet known which is a potential impactful issue.]

Are there any strategies at all that the firm can use to mitigate unknown-unknown risks? Unfortunately, these types of risks may create a mega-disaster that wipes out years of profit and may even force a company to exit a certain region or a specific market.

This section presents three methods for managing supply chain risks and, in particular, for managing the unknown-unknown. They are (1) invest in capacity redundancy, (2) increase velocity in sensing and responding, and (3) create a flexible supply chain community. A company that uses these methods effectively will have a *resilient supply chain* that allows it to recover from misfortune. Each method focuses on a different supply chain dimension. Capacity redundancy needs to be built at the design stage, speed in sensing and responding requires accurate and timely information, and a flexible supply chain community requires partners that embrace flexibility, work toward the same objectives, and benefit from the financial gains.

Capacity Redundancy

A key challenge in risk management is to design the supply chain so that it can effectively respond to unforeseen events (the unknown-unknown) without significantly increasing costs. This can be done through careful analysis of supply chain cost trade-offs so that the appropriate level of redundancy is built into the supply chain.

Example 5.2

In 2001, a United States–based consumer packaged-goods company had a global supply chain with about forty manufacturing facilities all over the world. Demand for its products (household goods) was spread over many countries. The company grew organically and through acquisitions. Management realized that it was time to rationalize its manufacturing network and close nonproductive manufacturing facilitates. Initial analysis indicated that the firm could reduce costs by about $40 million a year by shutting down seventeen of its existing manufacturing facilities and leaving twenty-three plants operating, while still satisfying market demand all over the world.

Unfortunately, this new lean supply chain design suffered from two important weaknesses. First, the new design left no plant in North America or Europe, thus creating long and variable supply lead times to key markets. Such lead times require a significant increase in inventory levels. More important, the remaining manufacturing facilities in Asia and Latin America were fully utilized, so any disruption of supply from these countries—for instance, from epidemics or geopolitical problems— would make it impossible to satisfy demand from many market areas. So how can supply chain design take into account sources of risk such as epidemics or geopolitical problems that are difficult to quantify?

The approach that this firm took was to analyze the cost trade-offs. These trade-offs are illustrated in figure 5.3, where the horizontal coordinate represents the number of plants that remain open while the vertical coordinate depicts the various cost components—including variable production, fixed, transportation, duty, and inventory costs. The top line is the total cost—the sum of various cost components. As you can see, closing seventeen plants and leaving twenty-three open will minimize supply chain costs. However, the total cost function is quite flat around

---

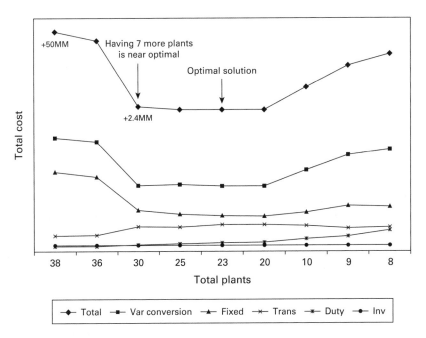

Figure 5.3
Cost trade-offs in supply chain design

Example 5.2
(continued)

---

the optimal strategy. Indeed, increasing the number of open plants from twenty-three to thirty facilities will increase total supply chain cost by less than $2.5 million and increase redundancy significantly. Thus, even though the risks associated with epidemics or geopolitical problems cannot be quantified, companies can prepare the supply chain for supply disruptions by investing in redundancy without significantly increasing supply chain costs.

The example above illustrates an important characteristic of total supply chain costs that can be used to build redundancy and mitigate risks without increasing costs:

Rule 5.2   *Supply chain cost is always flat around the optimal strategy.*

This implies that many supply chain strategies are close in total supply chain cost to the low-cost strategy but some are more effective than others from a risk mitigation point of view. Taking advantage of this property allows the firm to find the right balance between seemingly conflicting objectives—cost reduction and risk management.

The same property can be applied when the focus is on reducing carbon footprint. If environmental regulations such as cap-and-trade are considered, the firm can take advantage of rule 5.2 and choose a strategy whose cost is close to the optimal and its carbon footprint does not violate the carbon cap. This and other green strategies are analyzed in chapter 11, section 11.2.

Speed in Sensing and Responding

The following case illustrates how speed in sensing and responding can help the firm overcome unexpected supply problems. It also illustrates how failure to sense and therefore respond to changes in the supply chain can force a company to exit a specific market.

Example 5.3

In 2000, the Philips Semiconductor factory in Albuquerque, New Mexico, produced several types of radio frequency chips used in mobile telephones. Major customers included original equipment manufacturers such as Ericsson and Nokia. On Friday, March 17, 2000, at 8:00 p.m., lightning struck the Philips plant. The fire, smoke, and water used during the fire exhaustion destroyed or contaminated almost all the silicon stock in the factory, and the plant was shut down for months.

Three days after the fire, Nokia detected delays in incoming orders from the Albuquerque plant. In the initial contacts, Philips reported that it expected the plant to be shut for only one week. Fearing the worst, Nokia decided to send engineers to New Mexico to evaluate the damage. When the engineers were not allowed access to the plant, Nokia raised red flags and increased the frequency of monitoring incoming orders from the plant from weekly to daily. On March 31, two weeks after the fire, Philips confirmed to Nokia that months of orders would be disrupted.

Nokia's response to the news was decisive. The company changed product design so that it could use chips from other suppliers that committed to a five-day lead time. Unfortunately, this was not enough. One of the five components provided by Philips was impossible to source from other suppliers. So Nokia convinced Philips to provide this component from two of Philips's factories in China and the Netherlands.

Ericsson's experience was quite different. The news took four weeks to reach upper management, even though Philips informed Ericsson of

Example 5.3
(continued)

the fire three days after the incident. It took Ericsson five weeks to realize the severity of the situation. By that time, the alternative supply of chips was already taken by Nokia. The impact on Ericsson was devastating. Nearly $400 million in potential sales was lost, and only part of the loss was covered by insurance. This, together with other problems, such as component shortages, the wrong product mix, and marketing problems—caused Ericsson Cell Phone Division to suffer a $1.68 billion loss in 2000 and forced the company to exit the cell-phone market.[2]

This case can be put in perspective by reviewing Nokia and Ericsson's strategies prior to 2000. For many years, Nokia focused on modular product architecture, a strategy that provides supply chain flexibility through product design (see chapter 9). Because Ericsson's strategy was all about cost reduction, it adopted a single sourcing strategy in the 1990s—eliminating backup suppliers in an effort to reduce costs and streamline the supply chain.[3]

The implications are clear: supply chain cost reduction cannot justify a business strategy that does not maintain any degree of flexibility.

Rule 5.3 *Invest now, or pay later: firms need to invest in flexibility, or they will pay the price later.*

A Flexible Supply Chain Community

Ensuring a flexible supply chain community is the most difficult risk management method to implement effectively. It requires all supply chain partners to share the same culture, work toward the same objectives, and benefit from financial gains. It creates a community of supply chain partners that morph and reorganize to react better to sudden crises. The next example illustrates the effectiveness of a flexible supply chain community.

Example 5.4

In 1997, Aisin Seiki was the sole supplier of 98 percent of the brake-fluid proportioning valves (P-valves) used by Toyota Japan. P-valves are inexpensive (about $7 each) but important in the assembly of any car. A supply interruption would shut down the Toyota production line. On Saturday,

Example 5.4
(continued)

February 1, 1997, a fire stopped production at Aisin Seiki's main factory in the industrial area of Kariya, where other Toyota providers are located. Initial evaluation of the damage estimated that it would take two weeks to restart production and six months for complete recovery.[4]

The situation was critical. Toyota was facing a season of great demand, and plants were operating at full capacity, producing close to 15,500 vehicles per day. Toyota's production system followed a just-in-time principle that stocked two to three days of inventory at a time, giving its plants a margin of only a few days before they would have to come to a complete stop.

Immediately after the fire, Toyota and its suppliers initiated a recovery effort to restructure the entire supply chain of P-valves. Blueprints of the valves were distributed to all Toyota suppliers, and engineers from Aisin Seiki and Toyota were relocated to suppliers' facilities and other surrounding companies such as Brother—a manufacturer of printers and

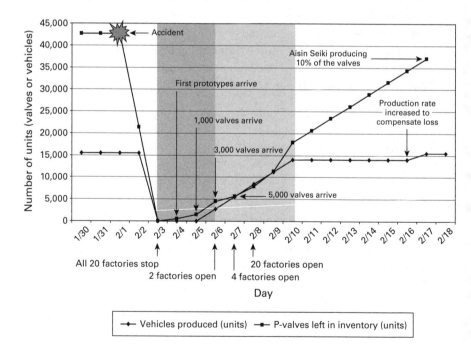

Figure 5.4
Vehicle production and P-valve inventory levels

Example 5.4
(continued)

---

sewing machines. Existing machinery was adapted to build valves accord-
ing to Aisin Seiki and Toyota's specifications, and new machinery was
acquired in the spot market. "Within days, firms with little experience
with P-valves were manufacturing and delivering parts to Aisin, where
they were assembled and inspected before shipment to Toyota."[5] All and
all, about 200 of Toyota's suppliers collaborated in the effort to mini-
mize the impact of the Aisin Seiki fire and help the Toyota production
line to recover as soon as possible.[6]

Figure 5.4 depicts the evolution of the production and inventories of
valves and vehicles during the crisis. Factories came to a complete stop
for three days, and full production was restored in less than one week.
The accident initially cost Aisin Seiki 7.8 billion yen ($65 million) and
cost Toyota 160 billion yen ($1.3 billion).[7] However, it is estimated that
the damage was reduced to 30 billion yen ($250 million) with extra shifts
and overtime.[8] In addition, Toyota issued a $100 million token of appre-
ciation to its providers as a gift for their collaboration.

This example illustrates how Toyota's suppliers self-organized to address
a sudden disruption in the supply of a key component. However, it raises
three important questions. Does a single sourcing strategy make sense for
such a key component? Even if a single sourcing strategy is appropriate,
shouldn't Toyota carry large amounts of inventory for such a low-cost but
key component? Finally, what underlying mechanisms in Toyota's supply
chain help the firm quickly recover from a sudden supply disruption?

According to Kiyoshi Kinoshita, Toyota's general manager of production control, single sourcing and holding almost no inventory were cal-
culated risks.[9] Toyota's single sourcing allows Aisin Seiki to achieve
economies of scale in P-valve production and offer high quality at very
low cost to Toyota.[10]

T. Nishiguchi and A. Beaudet discuss the third question in detail.[11]
They observe that key to understanding the ability of the supply chain
to adapt to the new environment is the just-in-time (or lean) philosophy
that Toyota and its suppliers followed almost religiously. The essence of
just-in-time is to keep work-in-process (WIP) inventories at low levels to
promote high quality and a quick identification of problems in the production line. In just-in-time, every worker has the authority to stop the
line to correct any problem, which fosters the company's problem-
solving capability (see chapter 8).[12]

These qualities were essential to the quick adaptability of Toyota's supply chain (example 5.4). As soon as Toyota identified that the Aisin Seiki fire was a problem, it stopped both its own production lines and the entire supply chain. This full stop of the chain forced supply chain partners to deal with the challenge.[13]

The Philips and Toyota case studies illustrate the supply-risk framework introduced in chapter 4, section 4.2. Radio frequency chips and P-valves are low-cost components whose disruption creates significant financial effects that need to be managed through inventory, dual sourcing, or flexibility. Product-design flexibility enabled Nokia to recover quickly from a supply disruption caused by the fire at Philips Semiconductor's factory, while process flexibility allowed Toyota to restart the supply of P-valves soon after a major disruption.

5.3 Managing Global Risks

Other risks faced by global supply chains include risks that, to a certain extent, can be quantified and controlled—the intermediate risks identified in figure 5.1. Bruce Kogut has suggested that a global supply chain can apply three strategies for addressing global risks—speculative, hedge, and flexible strategies.[14]

Speculative Strategies
Using *speculative strategies*, a company bets on a single scenario—with often spectacular results if the scenario is realized and dismal ones if it is not. For example, in the late 1970s and early 1980s, Japanese automakers bet that if they did all of their manufacturing in Japan, rising labor costs would be more than offset by exchange-rate benefits and rising productivity. For a while, these bets paid off, but then rising labor costs and unfavorable exchange rates began to hurt manufacturers, and it became necessary to build plants overseas. If it had remained favorable to do all the manufacturing in Japan, the Japanese manufacturers would have won the bet because building new facilities is time-consuming and expensive.

Hedge Strategies
Using *hedge strategies*, a company designs the supply chain in a way that any loss in part of the supply chain will be offset by a gain in another part. For example, Volkswagen operates plants in the United States, Brazil, Mexico, and Germany, which are important markets for

Volkswagen products. Depending on macroeconomic conditions, certain plants may be more profitable at various times than others. Hedge strategies, *by design*, are simultaneously successful in some locations and unsuccessful in others.

Flexible Strategies

When properly deployed, flexible *strategies* enable a company to take advantage of different scenarios. Typically, flexible supply chains are designed with *dual sourcing* and *redundant manufacturing capacity* in different countries. In addition, factories are designed to be flexible so that products can be moved at minimal cost from region to region as economic conditions demand (see chapter 7 for more on achieving flexibility through system design).

Example 5.5

A manufacturer in the apparel industry has a global network with six plants—in the United States (Florida), China, France, Mexico, Philippine, and Poland. Each plant is dedicated to one product family, and manufacturing capacity is designed so that line utilization is 90 percent based on projected demand. The firm sells its products all over the world in more than 100 different markets.

As is typical in the apparel industry, production sourcing decisions were made in the late 1990s and have not changed in the last ten years. This strategy focused on reducing manufacturing costs by employing a dedicated production strategy: each plant was responsible for one product family. Indeed, the high volume product family (accounting for about 20 percent of total demand) was produced in China (at a low-cost plant), while the low-volume product family (representing about 14 percent of demand) was produced in France (at a high cost plant).

This strategy worked well for quite a while. Recently, however, major retailers have been under a lot of pressure to reduce costs. This pressure emerged at a time when labor costs in developing countries have increased significantly. Some analysts estimate that in China, for example, labor costs in the manufacturing sector increased between 2003 and 2008 by a staggering 140 percent. Slowly but surely, a production sourcing strategy that worked well five years earlier had become ineffective. More confusing was the challenge to estimate where labor costs are heading and how much more expensive ocean transportation would become with highly volatile oil prices. Something needed to be done, but no one was sure what to do.

Example 5.5
(continued)

The planning team charged with the challenge recognized that any new strategy must take into account wage and productivity differences among the six countries. These data are presented in figure 5.5 which shows average hourly wage and gross domestic product per employed person for each country for the last fifteen or so years. Wages in France have increased relative to the United States, while productivity in France relative to the United States has decreased. China's productivity has increased in the last few years, and it is now more productive than the Philippines, while Poland is more productive but more expensive than Mexico.

To capture differences in wages and productivity for the six manufacturing locations, an index was created to compare expected per-unit costs of production in each country. The index uses the United States as a base level of 100. Table 5.1 shows that France is the most expensive labor-cost country and that China is the least expensive country. But the United States is only four times more expensive than China, while Mexico and Poland are less than twice more expensive than China. This is counter to figures typically cited by popular media suggesting that U.S. labor cost is at least ten times more expensive than labor cost in China. Combining wage and productivity shows a much smaller gap in manufacturing costs among countries such as Poland, Mexico, and China.

When the team began to analyze various options, investing in more capacity in low-cost countries was not one of them because of the increase in labor cost and the capital required. Outsourcing was not an option either. But flexibility was a real and attractive possibility since it

Table 5.1
Per-unit labor costs based on wage and productivity

Country	Cost per unit index
France	137
United States	100
Poland	53
China	27
Philippines	42
Mexico	41

Example 5.5
(continued)

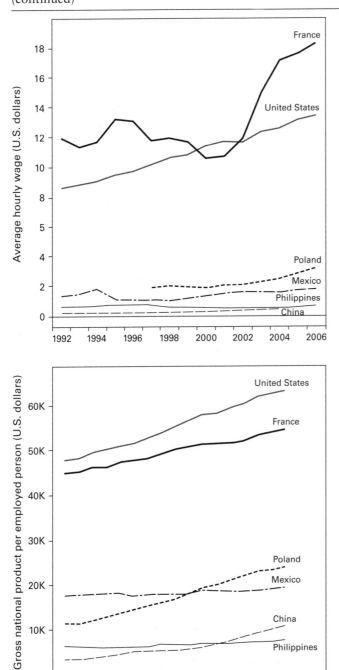

Figure 5.5
Wage and productivity analysis

Example 5.5
(continued)

does not require significant capital, it relies on available resources, and it provides a mitigation strategy against volatility in labor costs, oil price, and demand (see chapters 7 and 10). But how much flexibility was required and where to invest in flexibility were open for debate.

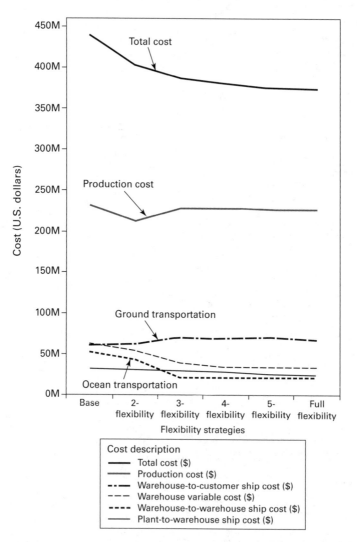

Figure 5.6
Cost comparison of six flexibility strategies

Example 5.5
(continued)

To *address these issues and to estimate the benefits of investing in flexibility in this global network, the team analyzed six different system design strategies:*

· Base case   *Each plant focuses on a single product family.*
· 2-flexibility   *Each plant can manufacture up to two product families.*
· 3-flexibility   *Each plant can manufacture up to three product families.*
· 4-flexibility   *Each plant can manufacture up to four product families.*
· 5-flexibility   *Each plant can manufacture up to five product families.*
· Full flexibility   *Each plant can manufacture all six product families.*

Figure 5.6 illustrates the ways that the various strategies affect each of the relevant supply chain costs. Investing in more flexibility reduces ocean transportation costs and increases ground transportation costs because more demand is served from local plants. Manufacturing costs first decrease and then increase as the firm invests in more flexibility. This is to be expected since investing in 2-flexibility is initially going to move production away from France and thus cut production costs. As the firm invests in more flexibility, manufacturing costs increase due to the loss of economies of scale. The net effect is that full flexibility reduces total supply chain costs by 15 percent. Note that investing in 2-flexibility provides the supply chain with 60 percent of the cost savings of full flexibility—that is, 2-flexibility reduces supply chain costs relative to the baseline by 9 percent.

Additional analysis was undertaken as wages rose in China and Poland and exchange rates fluctuated. The objective was to determine how well the new design, 2-flexibility, could respond to market changes. For example, the projected increases in labor costs for 2010 were about 20 percent in China and 10 percent in Poland. As expected, 2-flexibility outperformed the dedicated manufacturing strategy in this scenario, reducing the increase in costs due to rising labor costs by 15 percent.

The example thus illustrates three important observations that are often overlooked by management. First, operational decisions need to be frequently revisited, reevaluated, or simply changed. In a fast-clock-speed environment, decisions that were attractive and effective a few years ago may not be appropriate today. Second, production sourcing decisions should not be based purely on material or labor costs. Productivity plays an important role in the analysis. But even this is not enough! Senior management should consider the effects of various sourcing decisions on total supply chain costs, including transportation and inventory. Finally, volatility in oil prices, exchange rates, and customer demand together with the uncertainty about labor costs supports investing in at least a small amount of flexibility (more on this in chapter 10).

5.4   Resiliency Scorecard

A company that cannot embed risk management as part of its cultural and organizational fabric cannot manage risk effectively. One element in changing culture, driving collaboration, and achieving a truly resilient supply chain is the introduction of a companywide resiliency scorecard. The objective of such a scorecard is to identify gaps in the company's risk management strategies by analyzing the current state of the company's risk mitigation processes and comparing them to its goals.

Cisco is a case in point. Cisco—the leading supplier of networking equipment and network-management solutions for the Internet—provides a broad range of products, mostly configured-to-order, through a large number of manufacturing partners. With almost all of its manufacturing activities outsourced, the firm faces significant risks.[15] This includes risks associated with manufacturing sites, suppliers, components, and test equipment. To address these challenges, Cisco's *resiliency scorecard* includes four categories—manufacturing resiliency, supplier resiliency, component resiliency, and test equipment resiliency.[16]

The resiliency scorecard predicts areas with potential risk and therefore helps the firm to take corrective actions depending on the source of risk. For example, manufacturing resiliency measures the existence of alternate sites, qualified manufacturers, and delivery response times when a disruption occurs.

Similarly, insights obtained from analyzing a supplier's behavior—using financial information about public companies and correlating the data with supplier performance such as lead time or service level—allow the firm to develop a *supplier score*. A supplier score is much like a credit score applied by the financial industry to estimate the likelihood that an individual consumer will default on future payments. In operations, a supplier score rates suppliers according to the likelihood that they will default on future commitments—such as on time delivery and quality—because of financial problems or labor disruptions. Such scoring systems may motivate the buyer to purchase more inventory in advance of a (projected) supplier bankruptcy, to develop a dual sourcing strategy for all high risk suppliers, or to search for an alternate supplier.

In component resiliency, only those components that significantly affect revenue are considered. Such components can be high cost components but also can be low-cost components (such as P-valves) whose shortage will disrupt the supply chain. In this case, resiliency measures the percentage of standard components, nonstandard parts with substitutable components, single-sourced components, and sole-sourced components.[17] Sole-sourced components are the most risky as they represent parts that are available from only one supplier. Single-sourced components have multiple suppliers, but the firm has selected, for various reasons, only a single supplier.

Cisco updates the resiliency scorecard for products already in the market on a quarterly basis. For new products, Cisco updates the scorecard at key milestones during the product-development lifecycle.

An effective risk management strategy does not end with a scorecard. It must be complemented with teams that help tier 1 suppliers improve their operations and reduce risk with their own components, manufacturing sites, and suppliers.

5.5   Coping with Counterfeit

Globalization has increased the risk that counterfeit components and products will enter the supply chain—with severe consequences to the economy, public health and safety, and national security. For example, illicit drugs pose health risks to the patients who ingest the medications and loss of revenue to the manufacturer. Similarly, counterfeits of electronic and computer components used in warplanes, ships, and communication networks can cause fatalities in military operations.[18] Finally, fake clothing, fashion, and sportswear products cause severe losses for the consumer-product industry.

Despite efforts by various companies, industry associations, and the federal government, the problem is growing. For example, figure 5.7 shows a significant increase in counterfeit drug cases reported by the U.S. Food and Drug Administration's Office of Criminal Investigations (OCI) from 1997 to 2008. No one knows for sure, but experts estimate that up to 15 percent of all drugs sold are counterfeit, and in parts of Africa and Asia this figure exceeds 50 percent.[19] More important, counterfeit drugs can be dangerous:

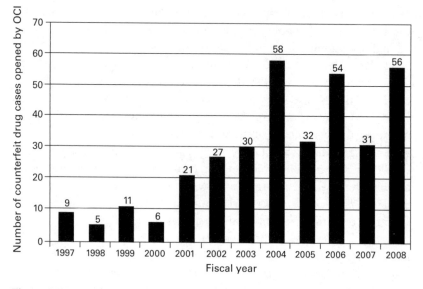

Figure 5.7
Counterfeit drug cases reported by the U.S. Food and Drug Administration's Office of Criminal Investigations. *Source:* U.S. Food and Drug Administration, http://www.fda.gov.

• In March 2010, thieves stole $75 million worth of prescription medicines from Eli Lilly's warehouse in Connecticut. Beyond the financial loss, the fear is that the drugs will reach consumers after being stored in clandestine warehouses, reducing their effectiveness, or worse, their content will be diluted with ineffective ingredient.

• In June 2009, the government of Nigeria announced that it foiled an attempt to import fake antimalaria tablets that were produced in China but labeled "Made in India." If the drugs were not intercepted by the Nigerian government, the lives of 642,000 adults would have been put at risk.[20]

• In 2006, more than 100 patients in Panama were killed by medicines manufactured with counterfeit glycerin.[21]

• In Haiti, Nigeria, Bangladesh, India, and Argentina, more than 500 patients, predominantly children, are known to have died from consumption of fake paracetamol syrup.[22]

• In the 1980s, 1 million counterfeit birth control pills were distributed to unsuspecting women, resulting in unwanted pregnancies and irregular bleeding.[23]

Counterfeiting is big business. The U.S. government currently estimates that counterfeits account for more than $1 trillion in annual business. In the electronics industry alone, experts estimate counterfeits cost at $100 billion to $200 billion annually, or nearly 10 percent of all electronic equipment sold worldwide.[24]

Fighting counterfeits requires a combination of technology and processes, but the specifics vary from industry to industry and even product to product. Before we identify the appropriate strategy, it is important to start with a definition of "counterfeit." According to *Wikipedia*'s definition (slightly modified here), *counterfeit* means "an imitation made with the intent to misrepresent its content, origin, or history." For example, in the electronics industry, a chip falsely identified as having been made by Xicor, a unit of Intersil, was discovered in the flight computer of an F-15 fighter jet at Robin Air Force base in Warmer Robins, Georgia.[25]

In the research for an article titled "Dangerous Fakes" published in October 2008,[26] *Business Week* "tracked counterfeit military components used by gear made by BAE Systems to traders in Shenzhen, China. The traders typically obtain supplies from recycled-chip emporiums such as the Guiyu Electronics Market outside the city of Shantou in southeastern China. The garbage-strewn streets of Guiyu reek of burning plastic as workers in back rooms and open yards strip chips from old PC circuit boards. The components, typically less than an inch long, are cleaned in the nearby Lianjiang River and then sold from the cramped premises of businesses such as Jinlong Electronics Trade Center."[27]

In the pharmaceutical industry, "counterfeit medications are deliberately and fraudulently mislabeled with respect to identity or source: their quality is unpredictable as they may contain the wrong amount of active ingredients, wrong ingredients or no active ingredients at all. In all cases counterfeit medicines are manufactured in clandestine laboratories with no possibility of control."[28]

There are various ways to combat counterfeits:

• *Supplier selection* As indicated in *Business Week*, the core of the problem in the electronics industry is that original equipment manufacturers purchase components from brokers and traders that are not able to distinguish fake from real parts.[29] This suggests that buying directly from contract manufacturers or authorized distributors is an important step in the fight against counterfeits. If brokers are needed, the firm may be advised (or required) to test each component.[30]

• *Marking*   Marking a product or a package in a way that is covert, is difficult to replicate, and yet allows quick and inexpensive identification of genuine products can help prevent mistakes.[31] Examples include holographic labels and materials with upconverting properties such as phosphors that emit visible light when exposed to certain frequencies of infrared lights.[32] In all cases, individual products or packages are not uniquely encoded, but the authentication of a genuine product is possible.

• *Encoding*   Saleable units, cartons, pallets, and other packaging configurations can be encoded using technologies such as radio frequency identification (RFID) or two-dimensional (2D) barcode (sometimes referred to as *2D data matrix*). RFID is a technology that deploys tags emitting radio signals and devices (called *readers*) that pick up the signals. The tags can be active or passive—that is, they either broadcast information or respond when queried by a reader. They can be read-only or read/write and can be one-time or reusable. They can be used to read an electronic product code (EPC)—a unique number that identifies a specific item in the supply chain—and to record information for directing workflow along an assembly line or for monitoring and recording environmental changes. An essential component of the widespread acceptance of RFID is the EPCglobal network, which allows password-protected access to the Internet of RFID data anywhere in the supply chain. A 2D barcode is a barcode that uses two dimensions (vertical and horizontal) to store data rather than the linear barcode that only uses one dimension (horizontal). This allows more data to be stored and is more difficult than a one-dimensional barcode to replicate.

• *Taggants*   Coined by Microtrace, the word *taggant* refers to an invisible material with a complex molecular structure that generates a unique fingerprint. Chemical taggants omit light that can be detected by scanners. These chemicals can be imbedded in various materials—such as labels, packaging, film, paper, and plastic—and provide a high level of security. Even when an adversary knows about the existence of taggants, it is difficult to decode the complex fingerprint produced by the chemicals. Originally developed to provide high levels of security and track-and-trace capabilities for explosives, taggants have been applied in other industries—like the pharmaceutical industry—and are incorporated into packaging resins, films, and inks for drug protection.[33] Its main limitation is the ability to scale because of the need for contact between the product and the reader.

A rigorous process for selecting and collaborating with suppliers is an important element in any anticounterfeiting strategy. But which anticounterfeiting technology should be deployed? Because each technology has its own advantages and disadvantages, companies need a framework to help them decide whether they should use marking, encoding, or taggants. These three technologies can be evaluated according to the following criteria:

· *Public health and safety* Taggants are the most secure technology, with unique product encoding that is difficult to break or replicate. RFID and 2D barcode are the next safest, although only sophisticated adversaries will be able to break into a supply chain protected with these technologies. The least security protection is provided by marking.

· *Cost and implementation time* RFID is the most expensive technology and has the longest implementation time. 2D barcodes and taggants require an investment in readers, 2D barcodes require tags, and taggants require chemicals and equipment.

· *Track-and-trace capability* Technologies that allow encoding have track-and-trace capability for identifying each product. This is true for taggants, RFID, and 2D barcodes. Track-and-trace provides records of the path that each product takes, not only within a company's supply chain but also between trading partners.

· *Scalability* Scalability is where RFID has the biggest advantage. Because there is no need for line of sight between readers and tags, individual products can be identified while still on a pallet. Taggants and 2D barcodes require pallets and boxes to be broken if individual products need to be identified at each entry point—warehouse, distribution center, and retail outlet. In addition, 2D barcodes are easier to scale than taggants since taggants need contact between the reader and the product. Similarly, taggants are customized for individual products, which explains the high level of security they provide but unfortunately this makes the technology difficult to scale.

· *Logistics efficiencies* Any technology that provides track-and-trace capabilities and scalability provides logistics efficiencies, since the firm can monitor in almost real time its inventory levels at different locations and can use this information to make manufacturing, distribution, or pricing decisions. This implies that RFID is highly attractive from this point of view, followed by 2D barcodes.

Table 5.2 compares the various anticounterfeiting technologies. Note the significant difference between 2D barcode and RFID. RFID can provide significant anticounterfeiting capability while the 2D barcode has a limited ability to do so. However, the cost difference between the two is huge. To put this in perspective, a recent MIT study suggests that

Table 5.2
Comparison of anticounterfeiting technology

	Encoding			
	Marking	2D barcode	RFID	Taggants
Health and safety	Low	Medium	High	High
Cost	Low	Low	High	Medium
Implementation time	Short	Short	Long	Intermediate
Track-and-trace	Not capable	Capable	Capable	Capable
Scalability	Low	Low	High	Low
Logistics efficiency	Does not exist	Medium	High	Low

for applications in the pharmaceutical industry, the cost of RFID tags needs to drop down to 5 cents per unit to justify using the technology at the stock keeping unit (SKU) level.[34]

The advantages and disadvantages of the various technologies suggest that the appropriate approach to counterfeits depends on product, industry, and level of sophistication expected from an adversary.

The Pharmaceutical Industry
The pharmaceutical industry has been perhaps the first to respond in a systematic way to the challenges of counterfeits. Recent regulatory and legislative initiatives include the following:[35]

· *U.S. states*   A number of U.S. states have established pedigree requirements. California has led the way, and by 2015 the state will require an electronic pedigree (see below) at a sealable unit level from manufacturer all the way to pharmacist.
· *U.S. federal government*   Congress is considering federal anticounterfeiting legislation.
· *International*   The World Health Organization (WHO) has established an International Medical Products Anti-counterfeiting (Impact) Task Force whose mission is "to promote and strengthen international collaboration to combat counterfeit medical products." In December 2008, the European Commission published its proposal on how to block falsified products from entering the legal supply chain of medical products.

A phased approach is needed for counterfeit protection in the pharmaceutical industry.[36] This phased approach has multiple objectives—to provide near-term protection for patients, to enable the industry to assume a leadership position and help shape future regulations, to create a flexible and financially sound base on which to build systems that will meet future regulation, and finally, to create a sequence of investments that will retain value as well as build levels of protection.

In this phased approach, the firm adopts a near-term implementation of a basic system of 2D barcodes for validation and authentication. An *exit point*—for example, a hospital, pharmacy, or possibly patient— uses email, text messaging, or Web access to send an item-level serial number (the 2D barcode) to the manufacturer (the *entry point*) for validation and authentication. An automatic response lets the user know if the serial number was created by the manufacturer. This point-of-entry/point-of-exit validation system is basic, simple to implement, and does not involve or put requirements on other participants in the supply chain. It provides near-term patient protection, builds company capability, and establishes a leadership position for future regulatory discussions.

Example 5.6

Roche India is currently using a variant of this point-of-entry/point-of-exit validation system, and Phillip Morris International uses this fundamental concept to combat contraband cigarettes in Europe. In the case of Phillip Morris, law enforcement agencies, retailers, and consumers can authenticate packages of cigarettes. For this purpose, a twelve-digit unique barcode is printed on the cigarette pack. The code can be transmitted and verified using telephone, text message, email, and Web sites.[37] In the case of Roche India, every unit of sale has a sixteen-digit alphanumeric security code, and text messages or emails are used for authentication.[38]

This basic validation system does not provide track-and-trace capability. As a result, it has some weaknesses and vulnerabilities, but it does provide a new, higher level of protection for patients. It also provides the foundation on which the track-and-trace feature can be built.

Adopting and implementing a point-of-entry/point-of-exit validation system is step 1 in a recommended phased approach. Implementing item-level encoding and providing validation at an exit point build important corporate capabilities and suggest solutions for the next steps. This step actively helps the industry shape its own future.

After regulations become clearer, the point-of-entry/point-of-exit system based on item-level encoding can be augmented to create and send an ePedigree message. An *ePedigree* is defined as "a record in electronic form containing information regarding each transaction resulting in a change of ownership of a given dangerous drug, from sale by a manufacturer, through acquisition and sale by one or more wholesalers, manufacturers, or pharmacies, until final sale to a pharmacy or other person furnishing, administering, or dispensing the dangerous drugs. The pedigree shall be created and maintained in an interoperable electronic system, ensuring compatibility throughout all stages of distribution."[29]

In this phased approach for the pharmaceutical industry, the investment in encoding software and hardware required for step 1 retains its value. In this upgraded system, the pedigree is created by the manufacturer and then updated by the manufacturer when an item is shipped. The pedigree then is sequentially updated as the item moves through the supply chain and tracks changes of ownership or possession.

The Automotive Industry

The level of protection required for supplier products in the automotive industry is not as high as in the pharmaceutical industry, and no anticipated regulations are being developed to shape standards and requirements. This industry is characterized by low margins, high volume, global supply chains, and multiple suppliers.[40] Unfortunately, RFID tags are still too expensive to be used in this industry, certainly at the product level. In this case, a hybrid approach is appropriate, so 2D barcodes or taggants are applied at the product level, and RFID is employed at the pallet or container level. This provides scalability at the pallet or container level and better protection at the product level without significant increase in cost.

The Food Industry

The food industry was one of the first to generate an interest in risk mitigation strategies, mostly for food safety. Since 2005, the U.S. Food and Drug Administration has required certain food facilities to maintain records identifying the sources, recipients, and transporters of food products.[41] The objective is to allow the FDA, manufacturers, and retailers to trace backward and forward food products throughout the food supply chain so that (1) the source of a compromised food article can be identified (the *backward tracing capability*) and (2) all food articles that emanate from the same source, are part of the same production lot, and possibly present a health threat can be identified (the *forward tracing capability*). Achieving such degree of protection requires the following:

· Using 2D barcodes, RFID, or taggants to encode at the carton or box level. Because of the margins and volume involved, the 2D barcode seems to be the most appropriate technology right now.
· Establishing unique standards across the industry or at least the product category, and
· Establishing shared databases so that the origin of a compromised product and the destinations of all products from the same production lot can be identified quickly.

Such unique standards and shared databases demand close collaboration among farmers, manufacturers, packers, distributors, and retailers. The industry is moving in that direction due to government regulations in the United States and Europe as well as early initiatives by manufacturers in Australia, New Zealand, and Europe.

5.6 Summary

There are many more man-made and natural sources of risks than those listed in this chapter. However, the principles presented here—including "Integrate risks into operational and business decisions" (rule 5.1), "Supply chain cost is always flat around the optimal strategy" (rule 5.2), "Invest now, or pay later: firms need to invest in flexibility, or they will pay the price later" (rule 5.3), and "Speed in sensing and responding"— are universal principles that can help companies mitigate many sources of risks, particularly the unknown-unknown. Of course, there are no guarantees that firms adopting these principles will always be able to overcome any source of risk, but following these principles significantly increase the likelihood of success.

Finally, information technology can provide track-and-trace capabilities for coping with counterfeits. But with IT investments accounting for a major portion of corporate expense, how should the organization set up priorities for its IT investments? How can the firm ensure that it is using its existing IT infrastructure effectively? Can IT provide a sustainable competitive advantage? These are the subjects of the next chapter.

Acknowledgments

Rule 5.2, "Supply chain cost is always flat around the optimal strategy," is introduced and proved in an earlier work.[42] Examples 5.3 and 5.4 were adapted with kind permission from Cela Diaz and other sources.[43] Example 5.5 is loosely based on my experiences with several companies.

The Eli Lilly story in section 5.5 is based on a recent op-ed article in the *New York Times*.[44]

Notes

1. The example is taken almost verbatim from D. R. Lessard, and R. Lucea, "Embracing Risk as a Core Competence: The Case of CEMEX," in *CEMEX 100th Anniversary Volume* (Cambridge, Mass.: MIT Sloan School of Management, 2008).

2. F. Cela Diaz, "An Integrative Framework for Architecting Supply Chains," MS thesis, Massachusetts Institute of Technology, Cambridge, Mass., 2005.

3. Ibid.

4. V. Reitman, "To the Rescue: Toyota's Fast Rebound after Fire at Supplier Shows Why It Is Tough," *Wall Street Journal,* May 8, 1997.

5. T. Nishiguchi and A. Beaudet, "Case Study: The Toyota Group and the Aisin Fire," *Sloan Management Review* (Fall 1998): 49–59.

6. Ibid.

7. Ibid.

8. Reitman, "To the Rescue."

9. Ibid.

10. Nishiguchi and. Beaudet, "Case Study."

11. Ibid.

12. See also ibid.

13. Ibid.

14. B. Kogut, "Designing Global Strategies: Profiting from Operational Flexibility," *Sloan Management Review* 27 (1985): 27–38.

15. J. O'Connor, "Supply Chain Risk Management," Cisco Systems, Inc., 2008.

16. Ibid.

17. Ibid.

18. B. Grow, C.-C. Tschang, C. Edwards, and B. Burnsed, "Dangerous Fakes," *BusinessWeek,* October 13, 2008.

19. R. Cockburn, P. N. Newton, E. K. Agyarko, D. Akunyili, and N. J. White, "The Global Threat of Counterfeit Drugs: Why Industry and Governments Must Communicate the Danger," *Policy Forum* 2, no. 4 (April 2005): 0302–0308.

20. S. Ogundipe, "Nafdac Seizes N32 Million Fake Anti-Malarial Drugs," allAfrica.com, 2009, available at http://allafrica.com (accessed on December 23, 2009).

21. "Counterfeit Drugs Kill," *IMPACT,* WHO, May 2008.

22. Cockburn, Newton, Agyarko, et al., "The Global Threat of Counterfeit Drugs."

23. "Counterfeiting Milestones over the Past Twenty-five Years," *ICC Counterfeiting Intelligence Bureau*, 2004; see also "Pharmaceuticals: Facts and Figures," International Chamber of Commerce, available at http://www.iccwbo.org (accessed on December 23, 2009).

24. R. Spiegel, "Counterfeiters Have Found a New Market in Parts That Component Manufacturers Have Discontinued," edn.com, April 9, 2009, available at http://www.edn.com (accessed on December 23, 2009).

25. Grow, Tschang, Edwards, et al., "Dangerous Fakes."

26. Ibid.

27. Ibid.

28. "Counterfeit Drugs Kill."

29. Grow, Tschang, Edwards, et al., "Dangerous Fakes."

30. D. H. Gray, "Counterfeit Products in the Supply Chain." Twenty-seventh Annual Government Contract Management Conference, Bethesda Md., November 20–21, 2008.

31. "Delivering a Counterblow to Counterfeiting," White paper, Microtrace, LLC, 2006.

32. Ibid.

33. P. Thomas, "Tuning In to Taggants," PharmaManufacturing.com, 2006, available at http://www.pharmamanufacturing.com (accessed on December 23, 2009).

34. D. Simchi-Levi, W. Killingsworth, and A. Sinha, "e-Pedigree: A Systems-Based Perspective," Massachusetts Institute of Technology, Cambridge, Mass., December 2008.

35. Ibid.

36. Ibid.

37. Comments by Philip Morris International on the "Public Consultation Paper in Preparation of a Legal Proposal to Combat Counterfeit Medicines for Human Use," May 2008; "Technology and the Fight against Illicit Tobacco Trade," Framework Convention Alliance, media briefing, 2008, available at http://www.fctc.org (accessed on December 23, 2009).

38. L. Joseph, "Firms Adopt New Ways to Fight Back," LiveMint.com, November 2, 2008, available at http://www.livemint.com/2008/11/02204451/Firms-adopt-new-ways-to-fight.html (accessed on December 23, 2009); and P. Reddy, "Roche Implements 'Mass Serialization' Anti-Counterfeiting Technology," October 16, 2008, available at http://spicyipindia.blogspot.com (accessed on December 23, 2009).

39. CA Business and Professions Code, sec. 4034(a).

40. M. Lehtonen, J. Al-Kassab, F. Michahelles, and O. Kasten, "Anti-Counterfeiting Business Case Report," *BRIDGE*, December 2007.

41. "Traceability in the Food Supply Chain," Department of Health and Human Services, Office of the Inspector General, March 2009, Report No. OEI-02–06–00210.

42. D. Simchi-Levi, "Hierarchical Design for Probabilistic Distribution Systems in Euclidean Spaces," *Management Science* 38, no. 2 (1992): 198–211.

43. Cela Diaz, "An Integrative Framework"; "Toyota's Fire Caused Production Cut at 70,000 Units," Japan Economic Newswire (via Factiva), February 17, 1998; Nishiguchi and Beaudet, "Case Study"; and Reitman, "To the Rescue."

44. K. Eban and J. A. Graham, "Are You Buying Illegal Drugs?," *New York Times,* April 1, 2010.

6

Rethinking the Role of Information Technology

In 1979, Kmart was one of the leaders of the retail industry with 1,891 stores and an average revenue per store of $7.25 million. At that time, Wal-Mart was a small niche retailer in the South with 229 stores and an average revenue per store of about half of that of Kmart stores. In ten years, Wal-Mart transformed itself and the retail industry, and in 1992, it had the highest sales per square foot, highest inventory turnover, and largest operating profit of any discount retailer.[1] How did Wal-Mart do it? The starting point was a relentless focus on satisfying customer needs. Wal-Mart's goal was simply to provide customers with access to goods when and where they want them and to develop a cost structure that enables competitive pricing.[2]

The key to achieving this goal was to make the way that the company manages its supply chain the centerpiece of its strategy.[3] Two major components in Wal-Mart's competitive strategy were critical to its success. First, an enthusiastic application of a continuous replenishment strategy initially developed in partnership with Procter & Gamble. In this strategy, goods are continuously delivered to Wal-Mart's warehouses, from where they are dispatched to stores without ever sitting in inventory. Second, to facilitate the continuous-replenishment strategy, Wal-Mart was the first retailer to invest in a private satellite communications system that sends point-of-sale (POS) data to its distribution centers and vendors, allowing the company to have a clear picture of sales at all of its stores.

Fast forward to 2008, this innovative company now lags behind the competition in its information technology (IT) infrastructure. It is loaded with home-grown rudimentary technology that cannot match what its competitors, Target and Amazon, are able to extract from commercial applications. And the differences show. In 2008, Wal-Mart's operating margins (5.73 percent) were lower than Target's (6.51 percent).

Wal-Mart ranked thirteenth in online sales volume and eighth in online customer satisfaction relative to Amazon, the king of the online channel.[4]

Wal-Mart is now competing with stellar retailers, both brick-and-mortar (Target) and online (Amazon), that invest heavily in IT infrastructure. Amazon has thrived during the recession, a period when some retailers had to shut their doors, because its IT infrastructure and supply chain efficiency enabled low pricing, broad selection, and quality services—the same dimensions on which Wal-Mart has built its reputation.[5]

Wal-Mart's remarkable journey suggests a few observations. First, IT in itself may not provide any competitive advantage. It was Wal-Mart's combined business processes (particularly continuous replenishment) and IT infrastructure (specifically, the satellite communications system) that enabled the giant retailer to do what no retailer has done before—reduce inventory levels and cut the cost of sales by 2 to 3 percent compared with industry average. This cost difference allowed Wal-Mart to offer everyday low pricing to its customers.[6]

Second, although IT is becoming a commodity that is available to any company from a variety of vendors, limping behind the competition in IT investment can have serious consequences on operational efficiency.

Finally, Wal-Mart's goal of providing its customers with competitive pricing was matched with its significant investment in IT infrastructure in the late 1980s and early 1990s. Its recent failure in customer service in online retailing is most likely related to a lack of investment in commercial applications that specialize in this channel.

These observations form the basis for the discussion in this chapter. Its starting point is the link between business strategies and IT investments, particularly the core operational capabilities that IT supports. I then argue that although IT is a commodity that is available to any organization, it is its combination with business processes that leads to competitive advantages. Finally, the chapter reviews some new developments that affect operations software and sets out a roadmap for IT investments.

6.1 Business Strategy and IT Investments

IT strategy should be driven by business strategy, not by a software vendor's newly released technology. Unfortunately, many companies confuse the two. IT decisions often are made by people who understand and are excited by new technology, advanced features, or rich functionality. These people do not necessarily understand the role of business strategy, and if they do, they are not always able to link or align IT with these objectives. Think about how many times you have heard in your own organization that a new technology for supply chain or operations was acquired by the IT department with little or no involvement from the relevant functional groups. When you raised questions about the wisdom of the investment, the response typically was, "You just do not understand. We need a technology that our IT department can support," and dismissed the need for technology that supports the business strategy and your functional needs.

So what should drive IT investments? *Is it all about being first to mkt?*

Rule 6.1   *Enabling, supporting, and enforcing a business strategy are the objectives of IT investments.*

The three key words in this definition of the objectives of IT investments are *enabling*, *supporting*, and *enforcing*:

Enabling   IT provides new capabilities that a firm was never able to accomplish before. Wal-Mart's continuous-replenishment strategy required a direct link between suppliers, distribution centers, and retail outlets. Without the IT infrastructure, this innovative supply chain strategy was not possible. Similarly, taking advantage of Amazon's investment in IT infrastructure, Target was able to successfully expand to the online market, thus providing a significant revenue boost.

Supporting   IT allows a firm to do what it used to do but more efficiently—at a lower cost, in a shorter response time, and with better service levels—affecting all the key performance indicators (KPIs) that are important in operations and supply chain management. Application software such as transportation management systems (TMS), warehouse management systems (WMS), and supply chain planning (SCP) systems are all designed and implemented to support existing functions and activities.

Enforcing   IT is applied to ensure that common processes and standard workflow are followed. For example, IT has been applied by Sony to automate customer-facing processes and improve those that require human intervention (such as approval, exception, and escalation).[7] Such standard workflow and processes are typically designed to guarantee consistent customer interactions, independent of the people and the manner in which the customer interacts with the firm, thereby improving customer experience.

Many executives fall into the *investment dilemma* when considering their IT strategy. Investment in new technology can be risky. The technology might be new, full of bugs, or about to be replaced and hence not supported in the future. There are also configuration, integration, and training requirements as well as investments in maintenance time and costs. By contrast, lack of investment may lead to loss of market advantage and, even worse, falling behind the competition. So, what should a firm do?

The answer lies in relating business strategy to the core operational and supply chain capabilities that IT needs to enable, support, or enforce. For example, when the business strategy is everyday low pricing, then cost reduction, supply chain efficiency, and supply chain planning are critical capabilities (see chapter 3).

If current IT is appropriately addressing these needs, typically no new investments are required. But when IT does not support core capabilities—perhaps because of antiquated technology, a change in business strategy, or new government regulations—then smart executives invest in IT.

Five core capabilities demand undertaking a deep and thorough analysis of a firm's IT infrastructure. Depending on their business strategy, companies do not necessarily need to have all these capabilities. After management determines the required capabilities, each will affect IT infrastructure and investment.

1. Supply chain collaboration and integration   In the next section, an analysis of data from seventy-five different supply chains leads to the conclusion that integration and collaboration provide the best way for companies to forge ahead of the competition and achieve significant competitive advantages. Such an advantage tends to be a sustainable one, despite pundits like Nicholas Carr,[8] who claims that "the opportunities for gaining IT-based advantage are already dwindling." To the contrary, a combination of IT infrastructure and business processes designed for supply chain integration and collaboration allows the firm to improve supply chain performance significantly on many key performance indicators.

Why have only a small fraction of today's companies achieved the level of collaboration and integration that provides a significant leap in performance? The answer lies in the inherent difficulties associated with supporting cross-company integration and collaboration. First, enterprise resource planning (ERP) systems such as Oracle and SAP (which typically form the backbone of most company IT systems) are not well suited for the task. They serve as a single point of contact within the organization but not across organizations. Even if IT infrastructure exists to support cross-company collaboration—and "cloud computing" may well be such a technology—this is not enough. Designing business processes that cut across organizations is difficult because of different organizational cultures, geography, conflicting objectives, and inflexible technologies (more on this in the next section). But when this is done right, the impact is enormous.

Consider Cisco, which in 2000 was forced to write down $2.2 billion of obsolete inventory when it was not able to respond effectively to a significant reduction in demand for telecommunications infrastructure. Many analysts and supply chain pundits blamed Cisco's business model, which outsourced manufacturing and focused on tight collaboration and integration with multitier suppliers. The wisdom and effectiveness of Cisco's strategy was apparent just a few years later. Competitors Lucent and Nortel, stuck with expensive infrastructure, suffered significant financial losses. Their combined losses in the five years following the 2000 telecommunications crisis was in excess of $57 billion while Cisco had a profit of $15 billion during the same period.

Depending on business strategy, the level of integration and collaboration differs from industry to industry and even from company to company. For example, tight integration and strong collaboration are critical in the high-tech field, where products are innovative and technology has a fast clock-speed. This is not the case for consumer packaged-goods manufactures, where products tend to be functional and their technology does not change frequently. These characteristics and differences lead to different IT requirements.

2. Centralized and decentralized decision making   In many organizations, some decisions are made centrally and others are made locally. This hybrid decision-making process must be enabled by technology. For example, in system flexibility (chapter 7), plants can produce multiple products, and the specific products that are produced by a plant change from quarter to quarter depending on market and business conditions. Such a flexible strategy requires supply chain coordination that dynamically allocates demand to the various plants to maximize system performance. After demand is allocated, the plants plan production—and sometimes distribution—independently of each other. This hybrid approach requires information sharing and effective decision support systems, both centrally and locally at the plants.

Zara, to give another example, allows store managers to make product-assortment and buying decisions so that stores are responsive to local needs. No centralized assortment or buying decisions are followed. As a result, Zara's IT strategy is designed to support this core capability: store managers have hand-held devices that are used to place orders for new products. But not all decisions are made locally. Pricing decisions are centralized using point-of-sales (POS) data transmitted to headquarter on a daily basis. For all these reasons, Zara's IT infrastructure is very basic, focusing only on providing these capabilities successfully. One implication is that Zara has no ERP system and does not invest in demand forecasting or replenishment technologies.[9]

3. Synergies across multiple supply chains   In chapter 2, it was noted that depending on customer value, the firm may need multiple supply chains. This is the case when the firm is supporting two channels (retail and online) or when it has a portfolio of products, where some are functional and others are innovative. But having multiple supply chains within the same company does not mean that they are completely independent of each other. Indeed, smart executives are able to take advantage of synergies between the different supply chains, including synergies in procurement, product design, manufacturing, logistics, and distribution.

Often, IT is the enabler that allows firms to take advantage of synergies. For example, by consolidating orders across the various channels, the firm can take advantage of economies of scale and use standard parts, thus leveraging the risk-pooling rule (rule 3.1). Indeed, if demand in one channel is higher than expected while demand in the other channel is lower than expected, components and products that are initially assigned to one channel can be reallocated, thus improving the ability to match supply and demand.

Similarly, different channels may consolidate through common fulfillment organizations, distribution centers, and carriers, thus reducing transportation costs. When General Motors (GM) reengineered its supply chain at the beginning of this decade by investing in a new strategy dubbed order-to-delivery (OTD), the company consolidated the order-fulfillment organizations for the various divisions (including small, midsize, and luxury cars and trucks). This consolidation and other changes to its supply chains cut average response time for a customized car from about sixty days before OTD to below twenty days after OTD. The move to OTD also reduced supply chain inventory by about 50 percent. All these changes were not possible without an IT infrastructure that linked the various divisions and channels.

4. Supply chain visibility   The four drivers of investing in visibility are efficiency, responsiveness, risk, and regulations. These should come as no surprise since they are consistent with this book's approach to customer value.

• *Efficiency* refers to the ability to drive down cost. This includes the pressure to invest in visibility to reduce inventory levels, improve asset utilization, or coordinate inbound delivery in a just-in-time or lean operation.
• *Responsiveness* refers to the ability to focus on speed, order fulfillment, and customer satisfaction. Examples include using visibility to reduce out-of-stock, decrease lead times, or improve on-time delivery.
• *Risk* refers to the ability to sense and react to supply chain disruptions as well as counterfeits entering the supply chain. Examples include the ability to anticipate shipment delays or suppliers' manufacturing and logistics problems, to ensure food safety, and to combat illicit drugs and counterfeit electronic and computer components, fake clothing, fashion, and sportswear products.
• *Regulations* such as ePedigree requirements (chapter 5) or sustainability requirements force industries—such as the pharmaceutical industry for illicit drugs or the chemical industry for hazardous materials—to invest in visibility.

Visibility comes in all sorts of different forms.[10] The various levels of visibility can be classified into three nested categories—shipment tracking, pipeline visibility, and track-and-trace capabilities:

• *Level I: Shipment tracking* helps companies improve on-time delivery, better coordinate production with inbound shipments, and increase customer satisfaction. For example, Procter & Gamble invested in tracking shipments from its plants in North America to retailers. The technology helped P&G improve on-time delivery performance from 94 percent to 97 percent.[11]
• *Level II: Pipeline visibility* is a more advanced level that allows the firm to better sense and react to all sorts of delays and disruptions. Here the focus is on the visibility to supply chain events and status. Examples are the visibility to suppliers' manufacturing and logistics events, such as when raw materials arrive at a supplier's site.[12] Visibility to supply chain status is concerned with inventory levels at various locations in the supply chain, current production schedules, and advance shipment notices.

Bakers Footwear Group, a fashion footwear retailer, invested in pipeline visibility to quickly deliver a large variety of the latest footwear styles from Chinese factories to about 260 stores in the United States. The visibility system is used to monitor container booking, delivery to distribution centers in China, loading of shipping containers, arrivals at the Los Angeles port, and various activities at distribution centers in the United States. Pipeline visibility helped the firm identify bottlenecks and delays in its supply chain. It also enabled decisions about inventory allocation and the quantities and style of inventory allocated to each store to be postponed until after merchandise arrives at the U.S. distribution centers. The technology reduced a ten to twelve day factory-to-store cycle time to five to seven days, reduced transportation costs, and reduced in store out-of-stock and markdowns, thus increasing profit margins.[13]

· *Level III: Track-and-trace* provides the ability to track a specific container, pallet, box, or product in the supply chain as well as trace it backward and forward. In backward tracing, the source of a specific product can be identified, while in forward tracing, all products emanating from the same source can be specified. This is a critical capability in a variety of industries, such as in the pharmaceutical and food industries (see chapter 5).

Table 6.1 compares the various levels of visibility. As expected, shipment tracking is a relatively low-cost option, while track-and-trace is significantly more expensive since it requires either 2D barcodes or RFID technology as well as sophisticated software (see detailed discussion in chapter 5).

5. Performance monitoring and optimization This is perhaps the one area that executives understand well. IT infrastructure allows companies to *collect* information throughout the supply chain, *access* any data in the system from a single point of contact (all available information can be accessed in one stop and is consistent independent of the mode of

Table 6.1
Supply chain visibility categories, benefits, and costs

	Shipment tracking	Pipeline visibility	Track and trace
Efficiency	Low	Medium	High
Responsiveness	High	Medium	High
Risk	Low	High	High
Regulations	Not capable	Depends	High
Cost	Low	Medium	High

inquiry), *analyze and optimize* to plan activities and make trade-offs, and finally *monitor* the status of the supply chain.

What is less understood is the need not only to monitor the current performance of the supply chain by tracking various key performance indicators but also to *predict* what is likely to happen in the near future so that corrective action steps can be taken. This suggests a need to complement key performance indicators (KPIs) with key performance predictors (KPPs). For example, monitoring KPIs such as inventory and service levels may suggest that no action needs to be made, but reviewing shipment tracking data may indicate that lead times are likely to increase, thus requiring either more inventories or suggesting the need to expedite shipments.

Similarly, insights obtained from analyzing a supplier's behavior, using financial information available on public companies, and correlating the data with supplier performance (such as lead time, service level, or quality) allow the firm to develop a *supplier score*. A supplier score is much like a credit score applied by the financial industry to estimate the likelihood that an individual consumer will default on future payments. In operations, a supplier score ranks suppliers according to the likelihood that they will default on future commitments (such as on-time delivery and quality) because of financial problems or labor disruptions. Such scoring systems may motivate the buyer to purchase more inventory in advance of a (projected) supplier bankruptcy, lead to a dual sourcing strategy for all high-risk suppliers, or start a search for an alternate supplier.

Cisco has gone a step further and developed a *resiliency scorecard* that includes four categories—component resiliency, supplier resiliency, manufacturing resiliency, and test-equipment resiliency. The resiliency scorecard serves as a predictor of areas with potential risk and therefore directs the firm in taking corrective actions depending on the source of risk. Cisco updates the resiliency scorecard for products already in the market on a quarterly basis. For new products, Cisco updates the scorecard at key milestones during the product development lifecycle. This is a systematic, analytical approach that ranks various sources of risks based on their likelihood and potential impact (see chapter 5 for additional discussion).

Rule 6.2   *IT should be used not only to monitor current supply chain performance but also to predict what is likely to happen if no corrective action is taken.*

6.2 IT and Business Processes

In addition to the investment dilemma that exists when considering information technology investments, a second dilemma that executives sometimes face is the *business process dilemma,* which emerges after a decision is made to invest in IT. The same executives who made the IT investments resist changing their business processes to fit the new technology, either because they believe they have the right processes and in fact "no one knows better how to run our business" or because they are not sure they have the right processes but are worried about too many changes at the same time. Whatever the reason, this can be a huge mistake.

Rule 6.3   *IT investments need to be accompanied by similar and considerable investments in the appropriate business processes.*

This rule is supported by a wealth of anecdotal evidence as well as a recent study[14] that analyzed data from about seventy-five different supply chains. The study suggests that IT strategy, sound business processes, and supply chain performance are strongly linked. Interestingly, the study shows that companies that invest mostly in business processes do better than those who invest only in IT and lack the appropriate business processes. Indeed, it suggests that investments only in technology without the appropriate business processes lead to negative returns.

Specifically, the objective of the study was to determine whether there are direct correlations among the maturity of the business process, the maturity of the IT infrastructure, and supply chain performance. Unfortunately, it is difficult to measure the level of maturity of the business process or the IT infrastructure that a company possesses, especially because different portions of the company's business can be at different levels of maturity. Even one division within a business may be out of balance if the maturity of the business process and the information technology do not complement each other very well.

Levels of Maturity in Business Processes and Information Technology
Heinrich and Simchi-Levi reports on an empirical study that applied two sets of questions—one to characterize the maturity level of business processes and the second to characterize the maturity level of information technology.[15] There are four categories of business processes:

Level I: Disconnected processes   Companies at level I are characterized by the proliferation of many independent processes. Companies are organized functionally with no or a low degree of integration. Supply chain planning is typically done for each site independently of other sites. At this level, there are no measurements, or measurements are not aligned with company objectives.

Level II: Internal integration   At level II, companies are organized functionally with a high degree of integration. Decisions are made through the integration of key functional areas—sales, manufacturing, and logistics. Common forecasts are applied throughout the organization. Documented processes are followed across the entire organization, and key measurements are used departmentally.

Level III: Intracompany integration and limited external integration   At level III, companies are cross-functionally organized. Organizations at this stage involve key suppliers and customers in decision-making processes. Decisions are optimized across the internal supply chain, sophisticated processes involve all affected internal organizations, and key suppliers and customers are included in supply chain planning.

Level IV: Multienterprise integration   Organizations at level IV apply multienterprise processes, use common business objectives, and have an extensive knowledge of suppliers' and customers' business environments. Collaboration links trading partners and enables them to operate as one virtual corporation. Finally, measurements directly link supply chain results to company goals.

The various levels of business processes need to be supported by a corresponding information technology infrastructure. These are the four different categories of IT systems applied in the study:

Level I   Firms at level I have batch processes, independent systems, and redundant data across the organization. The focus is on spreadsheet and manual manipulation of data for decision making.

Level II   At level II, there is shared data across the supply chain. Decisions are made using planning tools that apply data across the supply chain—such as a demand planning module that applies expert knowledge, advanced algorithms, and statistical methods for forecasting.

Level III   Firms at level III have complete visibility of internal data. Key suppliers and customers have access to some of these data—for example, forecasts are shared with key suppliers. Both data and processes are shared across the supply chain.

Level IV   At level IV, data and processes are shared internally and externally.

A company has a mature business process (or IT system) if the maturity level of its business process (or IT system) is at least three. Finally, the best-in-class-systems (BICS) are the top 20 percent IT mature supply chains. These are the 20 percent of the supply chains with the top system maturity level. Not all of those have mature business processes.

Maturity Levels and Supply Chain Performance

The empirical study offers some insights about the effect of maturity levels in business processes and information technology on supply chain performance.

Companies with mature business processes have lower inventory levels. Figure 6.1 suggests that companies with mature business processes have significantly reduced the number of days of supply of inventory, cash-to-cash cycle time, inventory carrying cost, and total obsolescence cost, measured as a percentage of revenue. For example, process-mature companies with top systems performance (companies with best-in-class systems that are process mature) were able to reduce inventory carrying cost by 35 percent. This leads to the second key finding.

Companies that only invest in business processes leave a lot on the table.   The study suggests that the right balance between processes and IT enable supply chains to reach best performance. For most performance measures considered, roughly half of the performance improvement stemmed from advancing the business process to a higher stage of maturity. The other half of the gain in performance was realized by using mature IT systems. As figure 6.1 shows, for each measure of performance, BICS companies that are process mature have significantly improved on the process-mature companies. Similar results are obtained for performance measures such as on-time delivery, fill-rate level, and order-fulfillment lead time (figure 6.2).

Improvements in certain areas demand IT investments.   Consider the fill-rate levels shown in figure 6.2. Note that only make-to-stock (MTS) companies are included since this key performance indicator does not apply to make-to-order (MTO) and assemble-to-order (ATO) companies. The figure implies that IT infrastructure provides a huge competitive advantage with respect to fill rate. For one participant in the research—a global toy producer that faces thousands of order entries a minute during the high season of its business, the fourth quarter—each order

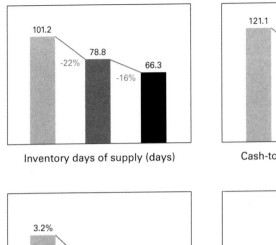
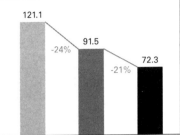

Inventory days of supply (days)

Cash-to-cash cycle time (days)

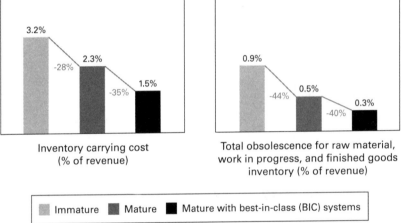

Inventory carrying cost
(% of revenue)

Total obsolescence for raw material,
work in progress, and finished goods
inventory (% of revenue)

Immature   Mature   Mature with best-in-class (BIC) systems

Figure 6.1
Mature-process companies have improved on inventory performance. Best-in-class system companies that are process mature perform even better.

has to be allocated to the right warehouse, and product substitution has to be taken into account. This environment demands a significant investment in IT infrastructure to provide the appropriate level of fill rate.

Investing only in IT infrastructure leads to significant inefficiencies. One of the most surprising findings of the study was that companies that have invested only in IT infrastructure but not in supporting business processes suffer significant inefficiencies. As figure 6.3 shows, companies with best-in-class systems (the top 20 percent of IT-mature companies) that are process immature have higher days of supply, higher inventory carrying costs, and lower profits than process-immature companies that

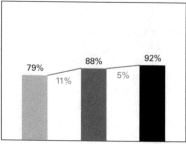

On-time delivery performance to requested date (%)

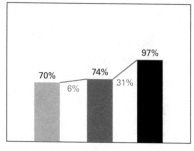

Fill rate by order (MTS only) (%)

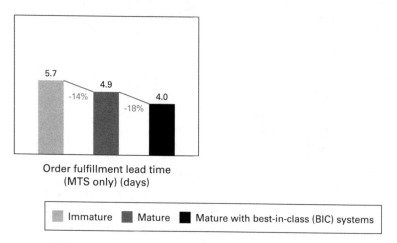

Order fulfillment lead time
(MTS only) (days)

Immature   Mature   Mature with best-in-class (BIC) systems

Figure 6.2
On-time delivery, fill-rate level, and order-fulfillment lead time

did not invest in IT infrastructure. For example, BICS companies with immature business processes have 26 percent higher inventory days of supply, 28 percent higher inventory carrying costs, and 7 percent lower average profits. The bottom line seems to be that implementing IT systems without the supporting business processes is a waste of money. *Priority in IT investments depends on your objectives.*   People frequently ask how various IT technologies affect different performance criteria, such as order-fulfillment lead time, inventory levels, or cash-to-cash cycle time. The study indicates that companies that support their demand planning process with a corresponding software module (a demand planning module) shorten their order-fulfillment lead time by 47 percent and reduce cash-to-cash cycle time by 49 percent. Effect on inventory levels measured in terms of days of supply is minimal—less than 10 percent

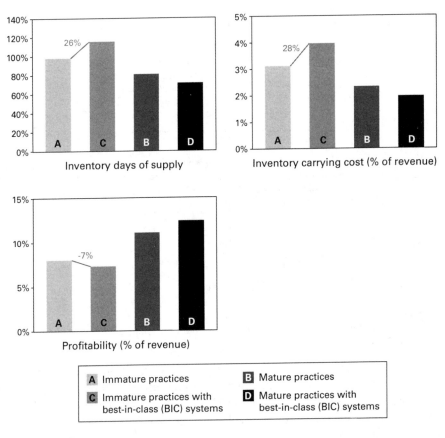

Figure 6.3
The effect of investment in IT infrastructure

reduction. On the other hand, supporting the supply-planning process with IT systems reduces inventory (days of supply) by about 40 percent.

This analysis is summarized in figure 6.4. The vertical axis provides information about the maturity level of the business processes, and the horizontal axis provides information about the maturity level of the IT systems. Box A represents supply chains that are characterized by immature business processes and immature IT systems. The study suggests that these supply chains suffer from below-average business performance. This includes high inventory levels, high cash-to-cash cycle time, and low profitability.

Box B represents supply chains with mature business processes and immature systems. Companies in this category perform significantly better than those that do not invest in either processes or systems, but they

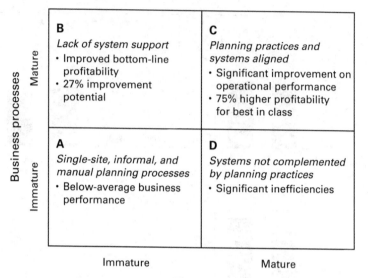

Figure 6.4
Linking processes and systems with operational and financial performance

leave a lot on the table. Specifically, the study suggests that these supply chains can increase profit (measured as a percentage of revenue) by, on average, 27 percent by investing in IT—that is, by transferring their IT systems through the stages of excellence to become mature systems. Such an investment in IT may require adjusting the business processes.

Box C represents supply chains with mature IT systems and mature business processes. These supply chains enjoy significant improvements in operational performance. More importantly, supply chain leaders— that is, supply chains that have mature processes and have best-in-class systems (are in the top 20 percent of IT maturity) enjoy 75 percent higher profits relative to other companies.

Finally, box D represents supply chains with mature IT systems but immature business processes. Surprisingly, the study reveals that these companies perform even worse than those with immature systems and immature processes. This situation requires more analysis. Everything else being equal, one would expect that a higher maturity level of the firm's IT systems would yield higher supply chain performance, but the study suggests that this is not the case.

To explain this dichotomy, observe that IT infrastructure typically requires significant investment accompanied by expensive support staff but provides only information. There is a need for a process that can effectively transform information into knowledge and decisions. Indeed, the role of the process is to ensure that the various organizational functions focus on the same objectives, that there is a single forecast and one plan that the organization is executing, that activities are coordinated and work is done at the appropriate time and by the appropriate people, that corrective actions are made before a disruption occurs, and that best practices are shared. IT alone cannot accomplish all of these objectives.

6.3   Lessons from the Last Decade

Today, the IT landscape looks vastly different than it did ten years ago. First, IT consolidation to a few players, each of which is setting its own standards, has occurred in all areas—from data storage to servers, and IT infrastructure.[16] Second, new sources of data (such as radio frequency identification and 2D barcodes) have received widespread support from technology providers, retailers, governments, and state agencies. Finally, new approaches to IT architecture and delivery, including service-oriented architecture (SOA), business-process management (BPM), software as a service (SaaS), and cloud computing have been embraced by IT vendors and users. All of these changes provide opportunities and challenges.

A review of some of the lessons learned in the last few years about information technology and implementation practices follows.

The RFID Experience

Radio-frequency identification (RFID) is a technology that deploys tags that emit radio signals and readers that pick up the signal. The tags can be active (they broadcast information) or passive (they respond when queried by a reader). They can be read-only or read/write and one-time or reusable. Tags are typically used to read an electronic product code (EPC), a unique number that identifies a specific item in the supply chain—not just the vendor or product family. Active tags can also record information to direct workflow along an assembly line or monitor and record environmental changes.

This technology, which at the beginning of the decade was considered to be the supply chain panacea, is not growing at the pace many of its supporters expected. Lack of common international standards, technical problems with tag-scanning accuracy, implementation complexity, and the cost of tags are just some of the problems that need to be addressed before the technology can revolutionize logistics and supply chain management.

Channel master Wal-Mart committed to RFID starting in 2003, but results are mixed. Today, only a small number of Wal-Mart stores and distribution centers are equipped with RFID readers, and a small percentage of its suppliers are tagging products. But where the technology is in action, the impact is significant. According to Wal-Mart, the RFID experiment with these suppliers reduced store out-of-stock by a staggering 30 percent.[17]

With this impressive performance, why is Wal-Mart's implementation so far behind schedule? The answer lies in the suppliers' challenges. Most of these suppliers, especially for consumer packaged goods, face low profit margins, and the cost of the tag (at least 20 cents) can erase all their margins. At the same time, to deliver store-level benefits from RFID implementation, tagging must be at least at the case or, even better, at the product level. Since tagging is done during production, suppliers have to tag all cases, even those destined to customers that do not require RFID.

So, the key lesson from recent RFID implementations is that the technology provides different benefits for retailers and for manufacturers. Retailers' benefits are in three areas—reductions in inventory, out-of-stock, and labor costs, even when the technology is implemented at only the case level.

By contrast, *high-volume, low-cost manufacturers are not likely to implement RFID, and if they do, it will be at the pallet level,* until the technology matures and the price of tags decreases considerably. This means that RFID benefits such as preventing store theft and providing the ability to read a customer's shopping cart—capabilities that require product-level tagging—will take a long time to materialize.

Apparel and fashion retailers are leading the way in item-level tagging in store RFID implementations. This is consistent with our discussion (chapter 2) of innovative products. Indeed, innovative products such as apparel and fashion items are characterized by high profit margins, enormous product variety, poor forecast accuracy, and high risk of obsolescence (see table 2.1). These characteristics demand a responsive supply chain (see chapter 3) that eliminates stockouts and increases sales. This is exactly where RFID makes a big impact.

In manufacturing, RFID has been used by innovative companies to improve visibility of reusable assets (such as containers, bins, and pallets). Initially, RFID was tagged to these reusable assets to increase utilization, reduce theft, and protect against counterfeits. As more companies have applied the technology to reusable assets, they have discovered that it allows them to improve operational efficiencies since visibility provides information on locations where containers are delayed as well as information on inventory imbalances. This information can be used to remove bottlenecks, reduce lead times, reallocate inventory to different stores, and in general improve supply chain performance.

Airbus's recent success with its implementation of RFID is an example of what visibility can accomplish. Its hundreds of suppliers are dispersed geographically worldwide, and the assembly of various parts is done in different locations culminating with the final assembly line. Coordinating the arrival of parts to assembly locations is therefore an important challenge faced by its supply chain. Airbus implemented RFID technology to track container movements across its supply chain, thus enabling the company to monitor the position, delays, and arrivals of parts to assembly facilities and to expedite the shipment of critical parts when necessary. This implementation significantly reduced the number of parts-delivery errors and the costs associated with correcting these errors. It also allowed Airbus to reduce the number of reusable assets (containers) by about 8 percent.[18]

The Emergence of Software as a Service

The Internet has created an opportunity for hosted software and services called *software as a service* (SaaS). SaaS is a software-application delivery model, sometimes referred to as on demand, where a software vendor develops a Web-native software application, hosts and operates (either independently or through a third party) the application for use by its customers over the Internet. Customers do not pay for owning the software itself but rather for using it over the Web.

SaaS is generally associated with business-application software and is typically thought of as a low-cost way for businesses to obtain the same benefits of commercially licensed, internally operated software without the associated complexity and high fixed costs required to purchase and internally install software. The SaaS model, thus, allows companies to convert IT fixed costs to a variable cost that depends on usage level and may vary over time.

This business model reduces IT investment and, more important, risk since it is easier to drop the technology if it does not provide value. The disadvantage of this model is that it does not allow for customization and therefore does not lend itself for a solution tailored to an individual company's needs.

Many types of software applications are well suited for the SaaS model, particularly in areas where customers may have little interest or capability in software deployment but do have substantial computing needs. Application areas such as customer-relationship management, video conferencing, human resources, accounting, and e-mail are a few of the initial markets showing SaaS success.

The SaaS model is particularly suitable for businesses that do not want to invest and support an IT infrastructure and for certain applications that require interactions with outside companies or across geographies. Therefore, many vendors, including SAP, are providing enterprise platforms on an on-demand model.

The most popular example is salesforce.com, which has been successful in the customer-relationship management (CRM) area. Applications that require connectivity with and collaboration between companies— such as supplier-relationship management (SRM) or transportation-management systems (TMS)—are natural candidates for this model. In fact, on-demand TMS is now estimated to be 33 percent of revenue from TMS and is the fastest-growing segment of this market.[19]

Another application that fits SaaS is collaborative planning, forecasting, and replenishment (CPFR), a Web-based standard that enhances vendor-managed inventory and continuous replenishment by incorporating joint forecasting. With CPFR, parties electronically exchange a series of written comments and supporting data that include past sales trends, scheduled promotions, and forecasts. This allows the participants to coordinate joint forecasts by concentrating on differences in forecast numbers. The parties try to find the cause of the differences and come up with joint and improved figures. Multiple forecasts can have expensive supply chain implications. Forecast sharing among supply chain partners can result in a significant decrease in inventory levels because it tends to reduce the bullwhip effect (appendix A). To do this, systems need to be designed to allow data verification and ensure standard practices of coordination.

The Impact of Business-Process Management (BPM)

Business process management (BPM) is an activity that businesses undertake to identify, evaluate, and improve business processes.[20] Business processes include a large number of rules (for example "If type A item stocks out, place an order for 1,000 units") and policies ("Keep two weeks of finished goods inventory for class B items").

Applying business processes effectively is a challenge. They are difficult to follow because of their sheer number. Lack of discipline can be the source of service or financial problems and even the source of operational risks. The business environment is changing dynamically, so there frequently is a need to adjust processes and rules. Different members of the same team (for example, those facing customers) may be applying different or even conflicting rules and processes. Finally, the need to handle a large volume of transactions, reduce costs, and eliminate errors may require combining and automating processes.

Business process management software allows companies to document processes, enforce adherence through process automation and business rules, and monitor and audit both human and system activities at all levels of the organization.[21] This transparency ensures that management is in the best possible position to identify operational problems as they occur, apply established processes to deal with common problems, and escalate those problems that are not addressed by established processes.

The following example illustrates the power of business process management. A major U.S.–based retailer sells products both online and in stores. Thousands of transactions are processed every hour—a transaction can be a sales event or a product return. Each transaction is checked for possible fraud or violation of the firm's return policy. The only way to do this effectively is by automating processes and requiring human intervention only when a potential fraud or return-policy violation is detected. Such an automated process must be accurate so that the rate of false-positive is low. Otherwise, the fraud-detection team will be loaded with cases that require manual intervention. For this purpose, the BPM technology was added as a layer above the retailer's enterprise resource planning (ERP) and customer relationship management (CRM) systems so that it could receive and integrate input from the various systems.

Because BPM technology acts as a single layer that cuts across all functional areas and different IT systems, it ensures that the organization can extract value from its IT investment. Indeed, it ensures that a single metric is used and that the various functional areas are focusing on the same objectives. At the same time, it allows workers to shift their attention from checking every transaction to focusing on those where manual interventions add value.

6.4   A Roadmap for IT Investment

In 2000, Nike invested $400 million in a new supply chain technology that, after a lengthy implementation, "cost Nike more than $100 million in lost sales, depressed its stock price by 20 percent, triggered a flurry of class-action lawsuits and caused its chairman, president and CEO, Phil Knight, to lament famously: This is what you get for $400 million, huh?"[22] Beyond software glitches and integration challenges, analysts believe that an important component of the project, the demand-planning model did not fit Nike's business model of a responsive supply chain.

In 1999, Hershey invested $100 million in new order-management, supply chain planning, and customer relationship management systems. When the three systems went live in the summer of 1999, major problems emerged. According to Hershey, at least $150 million in orders were missed, quarterly profit dropped 19 percent, and stock fell from $57 per share in August 1999 to $38 per share by January 2000.[23]

These two stories attracted the attention of the media and affected the companies' stock performance, but they are not unusual. Indeed, many corporations invest in information technology and later discover that some components in their IT do not fit their business model; that they use only a small fraction (typically 10 to 20 percent) of the software functionality; and that they have tried to accomplish too much and as a result failed in their IT implementation. This is not what corporate executives expected from their IT investment.

So with IT investment accounting for a major portion of corporate expense—and it now accounts for over half of American firm's investment in equipment[24]—how is it that many executives are disappointed with the results? The answer varies from case to case, but without exception, an important part of the problem is the approach to IT investment and implementation.

Traditionally, decisions about IT investments involve mapping out all IT projects at the beginning of the budget year and ranking them by their potential effect on the organization. A new IT initiative thus competes for attention and budget allocations from the management team based solely on projected return on investment (ROI). These ROI projections come from the IT vendor or from the corporation's IT team, neither of which necessarily understands the firm's customer value proposition or the link between this proposition, business and operational strategies, and IT capabilities—as is implied by the Nike story. After the initiative is approved, the implementation team typically focuses on features, functionality, and a comprehensive implementation to transform its IT and business environment (see the Hershey story), a big bang approach that may be trying to accomplish too much.

An alternative approach to IT investment is to consider the investment cost, risk, and business value across all IT projects and select a portfolio of investments that balances the three dimensions. If Hershey had enumerated the risks associated with the simultaneous implementation of the three IT projects, red flags would have been recognized by its management team.

Such a portfolio approach starts with the establishment of a cross-functional team that brings together IT, operations, sales, and finance. Depending on the objectives, operations may include manufacturing, logistics, supply chain, or transportation people. When IT investments target cross-enterprise opportunities (such as visibility and collaboration), the team should include representatives of the firm's supply chain partners.[25]

This team is responsible for establishing the business case and needs to align IT capabilities with business and operational strategies. Establishing the business case therefore demands a careful evaluation of the ability of the IT investment to enable, support, or enforce the business strategy. This step is not about new software or hardware or about an IT upgrade that provides "advanced" features, none of which is likely to be used—just as 80 percent of the features in the existing version are not used.

Instead, the business value provided by the technology needs to be characterized by goals such as reducing headcount, lowering operational costs, supporting growth, integrating the various business functions, and increasing business speed. Whatever it is, it must be aligned with the business strategy. For example, a sophisticated demand-planning tool is not appropriate for fast-clock-speed products, such as fashion, where the focus is on a pull supply chain. In such a supply chain, shipments are made based on realized demand, not forecast, which is likely to be highly unreliable.

Similarly, valuing ERP investments based strictly on financial returns is not appropriate since such an IT infrastructure serves as a single point of contact that allows the various business functions to access the same data, share the same information, and integrate activities. Therefore, ERP investment is all about quality data, compliance with government regulations, and business integration, which lead to financial benefits.

This step is also about selecting technology. Today, organizations have choices—from custom development, through off-the-shelf technology and SaaS, all the way to outsourcing (specific) IT capabilities to a service provider. Table 6.2 compares various options along four dimen-

Table 6.2
Information technology platforms

	Investment costs	Investment risks	Competitive advantage	Cross-company connectivity
Custom	High (fixed)	High	High	Low
Off-the-shelf	Medium (fixed)	Medium	Medium high	Low
SaaS	Low (variable)	Low	Low	High
Outsource	Low (variable)	Low	Low	High

sions of information technology platforms—investment cost, investment risk, competitive advantage, and the ability to provide cross-company connectivity.

As you can see, SaaS and IT outsourcing strategies change the structure of IT investments from an upfront payment (fixed costs) to a variable cost that is proportional to usage level. Such a change reduces costs and decreases risks. These two investment strategies rely on a third party and therefore are better suited for cross-company connectivity. By contrast, custom applications are designed to address unique challenges, and a specific business environment thus has the potential to provide competitive advantages. But such custom development is typically risky, exactly because of its uniqueness. Finally, off-the-shelf technology allows a new user to benefit from the experience of and share IT costs with other users that have purchased the software. Competitive advantage is created through an effective process that complements the technology (discussed in the previous section).

These advantages and disadvantages of the various IT strategies support a portfolio of platforms depending on specific business needs and value. For example, when the focus is on supply chain planning, off-the-shelf technology typically is appropriate. If, in addition, cross-company connectivity and visibility are required, SaaS may be appropriate because of the ability of multiple companies to share the same platform—see, for example, the discussion of the growth of software as a service in the transportation management system market segment. We conclude,

Rule 6.4   *A typical organization needs a portfolio of IT platforms.*

Finally, in the last decade, I have had the fortune to observe or be involved in IT implementations in various industries. Some implementations have gone remarkably well, while others seem to be in trouble right from the start, eventually providing no business value or even negative returns. A closer look at the various implementations reveals that the successful one always followed a few basic rules.

Rule 6.5   *Start simple, and add complexity later.*

Many IT implementations fail simply because the team is trying to accomplish too much too fast. The problem arises when executives and planners try to reinvent their IT infrastructure and business strategy by incorporating every business constraint, optimizing every business decision, and generating an alert on every exception or minor disruption—all from day one. This approach is supported by many IT vendors that are trying to capture market share as fast as possible. Unfortunately, this approach increases the likelihood of implementation problems and resistance to the system.

A closer look at successful implementations suggests starting with a small portion of the business that is enough to provide value, train users, develop training materials, and allow for learning and adjusting business processes. As the organization learns from the first implementation and success is communicated, stakeholders gain confidence, and new capabilities and additional businesses are added, typically based on a set of milestones that need to be achieved.[26]

Rule 6.6   *Do not fall in love with technology capabilities.*

Another common mistake is to define the implementation details based on technology capabilities. The more sophisticated the technology, the more it is tempting to take advantage of all its features and capabilities. For example, for many companies the implementation of visibility and event-management technology drives frequent adjustments and corrections. The assumption is that the more frequently the firm optimizes decisions, the more effective is its supply chain.

But this is far from the truth. Frequent adjustments of various plans may send conflicting messages and risk losing the trust of the organization in the process and technology. More importantly, each adjustment may be a sound one when considering the data available when the adjustment is made, but postponing decisions and observing more data may reveal that different decisions need to be made. Put differently, business characteristics should drive implementation details, not the other way around.

6.4   Summary

The objectives of information technology investments are enabling, supporting, and enforcing business strategies—not implementing new features, advanced capabilities, or the latest hot technology. These objectives are not new, even though they are often overlooked. However, IT investment is not enough. It needs to be complemented with the appropriate business processes. Our research shows that this combination of technology and processes provides a sustainable competitive advantage.

One complication when considering IT investments is the existence of various IT platforms. Although for many years, enterprise resource-planning vendors argued that this is the only platform that an organization should implement, smart executives understand that this is not the case anymore. Indeed, ERP systems do not support collaboration between companies; they do not facilitate sharing data across multiple partners; and some specific needs (such as strategic analysis, business-process management, and supply chain planning and scheduling) require custom solutions, a best-of-breed approach, or IT outsourcing.

The implications are clear. An organization should expect a portfolio of IT platforms to address all its business and operation needs and must consider a portfolio approach for IT investment. In such an approach, management must consider the investment costs, risks, and business value across all IT projects and select a portfolio of investments that balances the three dimensions.

Acknowledgment

Section 6.3 is partly based on a chapter by D. Simchi-Levi and E. Simchi-Levi.[27]

Notes

1. G. Stalk, P. Evans, and L. E. Shulman, "Competing on Capabilities: The New Rule of Corporate Strategy," *Harvard Business Review* (March–April 1992): 57–69.

2. Ibid.

3. Ibid.

4. T. Waligum, "Former IT Leader Walmart Loses Its Path in Web 2.0 World," 2009, available at http://www.itbusiness.ca (accessed on December 23, 2009);

"Customer Satisfaction Study Predicts Merry Outlook for Some Top E-Retailers; Others Will Struggle in 2009," The Annual Top 40 Online Retail Satisfaction Index from ForeSee Results and FGI Research, 2009.

5. S. E. Ante, "At Amazon, Marketing Is for Dummies," *Business Week*, September 28, 2009.

6. Stalk, Evans, and Shulman, "Competing on Capabilities."

7. "Sterling Commerce Helps Link Business Processes across Supply Chain," Sterling Commerce Case Study, 2008, available at http://www.sterlingcommerce .com (accessed on March 24, 2010).

8. N. Carr, "IT Doesn't Matter." *Harvard Business Review* (May 2003): 41–49.

9. A. Mcafee, V., Dessain, and A. Sjoman, "Zara: IT for Fast Fashion," Harvard Business School, Case 9-604-081, 2004.

10. B. Enslow, "The Supply Chain Visibility Roadmap," The Aberdeen Group, November 2006, available at http://www.aberdeen.com (accessed on December 23, 2009).

11. Ibid.

12. Ibid.

13. Ibid.

14. C. E. Heinrich and D. Simchi-Levi, "Do IT Investments Really Change Financial Performance?," *Supply Chain Management Review* (May 2005).

15. Ibid.

16. "Strong Growth Projected for IT Consolidation Market," Hewlett-Packard press release, June 2006, available at http://www.hp.com (accessed on December 23, 2009).

17. Waligum, "Former IT Leader Walmart Loses Its Path."

18. "The Smarter Supply Chain of the Future: Global Chief Supply Chain Officer Study," IBM, 2009, available at http://www-935.ibm.com (accessed on December 23, 2009).

19. E. Traudt and A. Konary. "2005 Software as a Service Taxonomy and Research Guide," IDC Research Report, June 2005, p. 7.

20. Definition for *business process management* (BPM) is available at businessdictionary.com.

21. L. Mooney, "BPM & EA: Two Smart Investments in a Recession," Metastorm.com, 2009, available at http://www.btpaustralia.com (accessed on December 23, 2009).

22. C. Koch, "Nike Rebounds: How (and Why) Nike Recovered from Its Supply Chain Disaster," cio.com, 2008, available at http://www.cio.com (accessed on December 23, 2009).

23. D. Gilmore, "The Greatest Supply Chain Disasters of All Time," *Supply Chain Digest* (May 2009), available at http://www.scdigest.com (accessed on December 23, 2009).

24. "Back to the Circuit Board," *The Economist* (October 22, 2009), available at http://www.economist.com (accessed on December 23, 2009).

25. Enslow, "The Supply Chain Visibility Roadmap."

26. Ibid.

27. D. Simchi-Levi and E. Simchi-Levi, "Supply Chain Management Technologies," in *The Handbook of Technology Management*, vol. II, part 1, ed. H. Bidgoli (New York: Wiley, 2009), 206–219.

II

Flexibility: The Key Enabler

7

System Flexibility

This book thus far has focused on issues that are strategic in nature—the alignment of customer values, markets, and channels with operations and procurement strategies; effective supply contracts that create value; risk mitigation strategies; and the link between business strategy and IT investments. These broad topics are important for any organization.

But details matter, and applying the rules, concepts, frameworks, and ideas described in these chapters requires more information. This is particularly true with respect to flexibility, an important theme that runs throughout the previous chapters and topics.

The need for flexibility is not new. Many of today's corporate executives have been influenced by Michael Hammer and James Champy's seminal 1993 book *Reengineering the Corporation*.[1] In their opening chapter, the authors observe that "Not a company in the country exists whose management doesn't say, at least for public consumption, that it wants an organization flexible enough to adjust quickly to changing market conditions." This observation still holds today.

Why, then, do many companies fail to meet customers' ever changing expectations, face great financial losses when there is an even the slightest supply disruption, or entirely collapse when faced with operational problems?

My experience is that most companies do not understand flexibility. They do not know how to measure the degree of flexibility in their business; how much (additional) flexibility they need, how they can achieve it, what will be the cost, and what are the potential benefits. For many corporate executives, flexibility is just another buzz word (like agility and resilience), at best used to provide an insight, not to make important business decisions.

Those who do understand flexibility, however, have applied it as a powerful tool to gain competitive advantage, reduce costs, and improve responsiveness. Indeed, at the heart of established business strategies—Toyota's lean manufacturing, Dell's direct-to-consumer, or Amazon's efficient fulfillment system—is a flexible operation that is designed to match the firm's business model and customer value proposition.

So what exactly is flexibility? Following D. Upton, I define flexibility as the *ability to respond to change without increasing operational and supply chain costs and with little or no delay in response time*.[2] In this definition, *change* refers to change in demand volume and mix, commodity prices, labor costs, exchange rates, technology, equipment availability, market conditions, or the production and logistics environment.

This definition includes three key words—*change, cost*, and *time*—that refer to the three most critical performance measures influenced by operations—customer experience, operational costs, and business response time. The "ability to respond to change" implies that even in the face of a disruption the firm should be able to match supply and demand to avoid hurting customer experience. Similarly, everything else being equal, implementing flexibility should help the firm reduce long-run operational costs or improve response time or both.

So how can the firm achieve flexibility, and how much flexibility is required? The last question is particularly important since flexibility does not come free. Typically, the higher the degree of flexibility, the more expensive it is to achieve it. Consequently, organizations need a systematic process to measure the level of flexibility that currently exists in their business, identify additional degrees of flexibility possible in their business, and characterize the costs and benefits associated with each one so that they can choose the best course of action.

These are precisely the topics covered in this and the following two chapters. Our approach is an engineering systems approach because it takes a holistic view of the business; it integrates manufacturing, logistics, transportation, and product design and hence is interdisciplinary; and it focuses on reducing system, process, and product complexity.

This chapter focuses on achieving flexibility through system design—a design of the manufacturing and distribution network that enables flexibility. The material is complemented with a discussion of organizational structure and business processes that support system flexibility.

7.1   The Concept

System design has the most influence on a company's capabilities and provides the most opportunities for leveraging flexibility. But how does one achieve system flexibility? What guidelines should the business

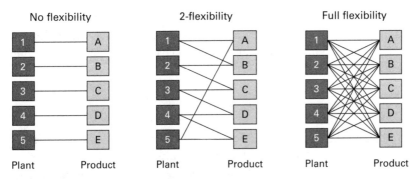

Figure 7.1
Achieving flexibility through system design

follow? These are important questions because flexibility is costly and changing system designs is difficult since it often involves assets such as plants, warehouses, and production equipment.

Following W. C. Jordan and S. C. Graves, figure 7.1 depicts three different system designs of a supply chain with five manufacturing facilities and five product families.[3] In the design called "No flexibility" (sometimes called "Dedicated"), each plant is responsible for one product family. By contrast, the system design called "Full flexibility" (sometimes called "Total flexibility") has each plant capable of producing all product families.

Under a no flexibility design, each plant is responsible for one product family, and hence lot sizes are large and there are no, or very few, setups. As a result, this system design reduces manufacturing costs. But, since each plant is focused on one product family, plants typically are far from market demand, which increases transportation costs. The reverse is true for a full flexibility design. In this case, each plant is responsible for many product families, hence lot sizes are small and there are many set-ups which increase manufacturing costs. However, market demand can be served from the closest plant, and therefore this system design significantly reduces transportation costs.

Between these two extremes there are various designs. For instance, a 2-flexibility design (the center design in figure 7.1) has each plant produce exactly two product families. Such a design increases manufacturing costs but decreases transportation costs relative to the costs associated with a dedicated, or no flexibility strategy.

Thus, an *n*-flexibility strategy is one where each plant is capable of producing *n* product families. The higher the value of *n*, the higher the degree of flexibility, and with this come different manufacturing and transportation trade-offs. Lower degrees of flexibility tend to reduce manufacturing costs but increase transportation costs, while higher degrees of flexibility reduce transportation costs at the expense of manufacturing costs.

7.2   The Impact

To illustrate how flexibility affects performance, consider the following hypothetical case that involves a manufacturer in the food and beverage industry. Currently, each of the five product families is manufactured in one of five domestic plants, and manufacturing capacity is in place to target 90 percent line efficiency for forecast demand. The objective of this project is threefold:

· Determine the cost benefits of flexibility to the supply chain,
· Determine the appropriate level of flexibility, and
· Determine the benefit that flexibility provides if demand differs from forecast.

To accomplish these goals, more information is needed about the current supply chain. Labor costs vary from plant to plant and depend mostly on plant location. Plant locations and average labor cost are as follows:

· Pittsburgh, Pennsylvania—$12.33 per hour
· Dayton, Ohio—$10.64 per hour
· Amarillo, Texas—$10.80 per hour
· Omaha, Nebraska—$12.41 per hour
· Modesto, California—$16.27 per hour

The firm produces to stock and keeps inventory at eight distribution centers located in Baltimore, Chattanooga, Chicago, Dallas, Des Moines, Los Angeles, Sacramento, and Tampa. Demand is closely proportional to population density but is highly uncertain, and the marketing department generated a forecast as well as a few scenarios illustrating that demand can be quite different from the forecast. Finally, inbound (to the warehouses) transportation is carried mostly through full truckload carriers, while outbound (from the warehouses) is done through less-than-truckload carriers and a private fleet.

The current strategy is focused on reducing manufacturing costs. The high volume product is produced at the low cost plant in Dayton, while the low volume product is produced at the Modesto plant, a high cost manufacturing facility.

The benefits of investing in flexibility can be estimated by analyzing five different systems:

· *Dedicated manufacturing*   This is the baseline where each plant focuses on a single product family.
· *2-flexibility*   This is a minimal investment in flexibility where each plant can manufacture up to two product families.
· *3-flexibility*   Each plant can manufacture up to three product families.
· *4-flexibility*   Each plant can manufacture up to four product families.
· *Full flexibility*   Each plant can manufacture all five product families.

Figure 7.2 presents a detailed comparison of annual costs for the various degrees of flexibility. As the degree of flexibility is increased, transportation cost decreases and manufacturing cost increases. Total cost is reduced with flexibility. This is not surprising since so far the capital investment required to achieve any degree of flexibility has not been included.

Observe also that full flexibility reduces supply chain costs by a total of 13 percent. Surprisingly, 2-flexibility captures 80 percent of the benefit of full flexibility because total supply chain costs, as a function of the degree of flexibility, exhibit decreasing marginal returns.

Rule 7.1   *A small investment in flexibility can significantly reduce total supply chain costs.*

Unfortunately, forecast accuracy for this company is poor. The question then is, how will 2-flexibility perform if realized demand is different than the forecast? It may be effective from a cost point of view but not necessarily as a tool to respond to change in demand relative to the forecast.

To address this question, we perform sensitivity analysis of supply chain performance to changes in demand above and below the forecast. For this purpose, three different demand scenarios are considered:

· *Demand scenario 1:* Growth for the two leading products by 25 percent and a 5 percent decrease in demand for other products,
· *Demand scenario 2:* Growth for the low volume products by 35 percent and a 5 percent decrease in demand for other products, and
· *Demand scenario 3:* Growth of demand for the high potential product by 100 percent and a 10 percent decrease in demand for all other products.

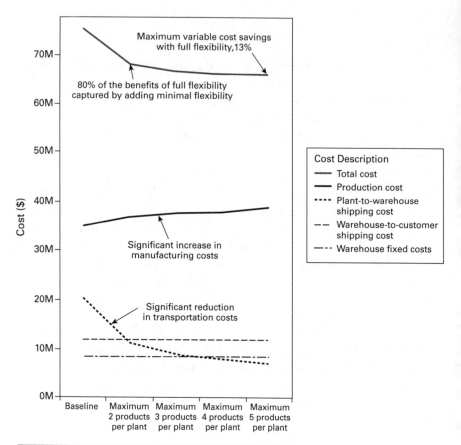

Figure 7.2
Total cost comparison of five system designs

Cost Description	Baseline	Max 2 products per plant	Max 3 products per plant	Max 4 products per plant	Max 5 products per plant
Production cost	34,960,649	36,730,087	36,639,959	37,913,955	38,830,279
Plant-to-warehouse shipping cost	20,264,858	11,225,563	8,895,809	8,006,541	6,908,562
Warehouse-to-customer shipping cost	11,751,467	11,692,662	11,722,858	11,743,225	11,773,756
Warehouse fixed costs	8,400,000	8,400,000	8,400,000	8,400,000	8,400,000
Total cost	75,376,974	68,048,313	66,658,625	66,063,721	65,912,597

Table 7.1
The impact of changes in demand volume

	System design	Demand satisfied	Shortfall	Cost per unit	Average plant utilization
Demand scenario 1	Baseline	25,520,991	1,505,542	$2.94	91%
	Minimum flexibility	27,026,533	0	$2.75	97%
Demand scenario 2	Baseline	25,019,486	1,957,403	$2.99	91%
	Minimum flexibility	26,976,889	0	$2.75	96%
Demand scenario 3	Baseline	23,440,773	4,380,684	$2.93	84%
	Minimum flexibility	27,777,777	43,680	$2.79	100%

Table 7.1 summarizes the effect of changes in demand volume on system performance for both the baseline and the optimal design of 2-flexibility (min flexibility). As you can see, 2-flexibility outperforms the baseline on every category and in every demand scenario. For example, in the first demand scenario, 2-flexibility satisfies more demand, eliminates the shortfall, cuts cost per unit, and significantly increases plant utilization.

At first glance, it may be surprising to see that in the baseline the shortfall is high but plant utilization is typically low. This is explained as follows. Although the baseline and 2-flexibility have the same aggregate capacity, the baseline does not have the right capacity allocation between the different product families.

Interestingly, 2-flexibility is able to perform significantly better than the baseline in every scenario, even though the design of 2-flexibility was done *independently of the various scenarios*. Thus, there is a need for a better understanding of why 2-flexibility is so effective. Such an understanding will provide operations and supply chain managers with design guidelines.

For this purpose, consider figure 7.3. The left-hand side presents capacity allocation in the baseline (top) and 2-flexibility (bottom). In the 2-flexibility strategy, the Pittsburgh plant is responsible for products 2 and 3, Omaha for products 2 and 5, and so on.

The same structure is depicted on the right-hand side of figure 7.3, where a link represents an assignment of a product to a plant. But this time, the design of 2-flexibility creates a chain that connects all the plants and the products either directly or indirectly. It is this *long chain* that

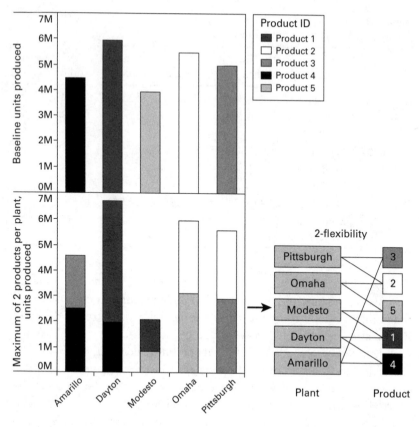

Figure 7.3
The power of 2-flexibility to provide full flexibility through a long chain

allows the supply chain to respond effectively to changes in demand volume and mix.

To test this hypothesis, compare two different designs of 2-flexibility (see figure 7.3). The top design is the 2-flexibility strategy described earlier. The bottom one is a different strategy in which each plant is still producing two product families, but now two small chains exist—one that includes Pittsburgh, Omaha, product 2, and product 3 and a second that includes all remaining products and plants. This design has the same number of product-plant connections as in the top design, but now the long chain is broken into two smaller ones.

Table 7.2 compares the effectiveness of the two 2-flexibility designs in each of the three scenarios described earlier. The original 2-flexibility strategy that creates a long chain either performs as well as the second

Table 7.2
Comparing designs with one long chain versus two short chains

	System design	Demand satisfied	Shortfall	Cost per unit	Average plant utilization
Demand scenario 1	Long chain	27,026,533	0	$2.75	97%
	Short chains	27,026,533	0	$2.76	93%
Demand scenario 2	Long chain	26,976,889	0	$2.75	96%
	Short chains	26,022,490	954,399	$2.79	94%
Demand scenario 3	Long chain	27,777,777	43,680	$2.75	100%
	Short chains	24,633,440	3,188,017	$2.66	86%

design or dominates it, depending on the scenario and the performance measure.

The effectiveness of the long chain can be explained as follows. Consider a scenario where all plants are operating at capacity and assume that demand for product family 3 increased by exactly one unit while demand for product 1 decreased by the same amount. In the long chain design of figure 7.4 (top design), the manufacturing network can still satisfy demand for product 3 even though the plants producing product 3 (Pittsburgh and Amarillo) were at capacity prior to the sudden increase in demand. This is true since the long chain implies the following cascading effect: the decrease in demand for product 1 allows increasing the amount of product 4 produced in Dayton, which in turn reduces the amount of product 4 produced in Amarillo, and hence Amarillo can produce one additional unit of product 3 and therefore satisfy demand. This is not possible in the two short chains design of figure 7.4 (bottom design) since there is no chain connecting product 1 to product 3.

To summarize, a chain is a group of products and plants that are all connected directly or indirectly. Long chains perform better than many short chains because they pool more plants and products and thus deal with uncertainty more effectively than short chains.

Rule 7.2   *A long chain is preferred when designing the manufacturing network for flexibility.*

In the case study just analyzed, the firm determined the appropriate level of flexibility by generating a list of demand scenarios and analyzing

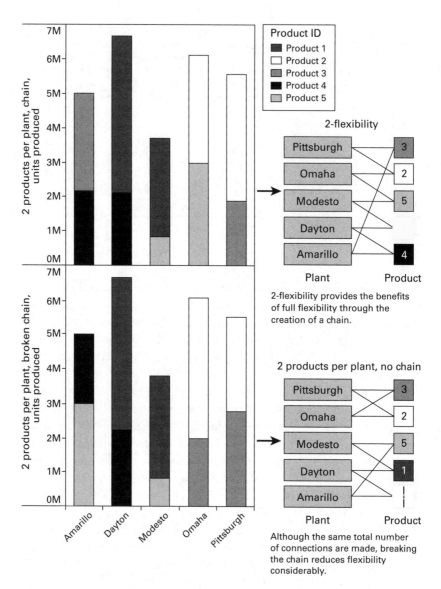

Figure 7.4
Two 2-flexibility designs: One with a long chain and the second with two smaller chains

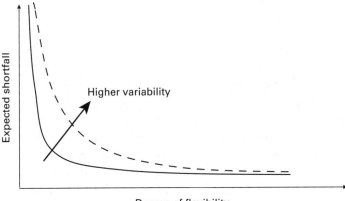

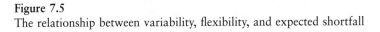

Degree of flexibility

Figure 7.5
The relationship between variability, flexibility, and expected shortfall

the effectiveness of various flexibility investments in each scenario. In many real-world situations, however, it is difficult to generate such a representative list. In these cases, scenarios can be replaced by varying the level demand variability and determining the performance of various flexibility investments against each level of demand variability.

So what is the appropriate level of flexibility that the organization must strive to achieve? Should the firm be able to respond to an unexpected increase in demand by 10, 20, 30 or even higher percentage points? The answer lies in the relationship between flexibility, variability, and expected shortfall, a relationship depicted in figure 7.5.

Observe that given a specific degree of flexibility, the shortfall increases with demand variability. Similarly, for a given level of variability, the shortfall decreases with the degree of flexibility. More specifically, for a given level of variability, the investment in flexibility provides decreasing marginal return. By comparing the investment in flexibility to the profit impact due to shortfall reduction, the firm can identify the breakeven point where any additional degree of flexibility yields negative return on investment. We conclude,

Rule 7.3 *Variability degrades the performance of the supply chain while flexibility improves its performance.*

7.3   Flexible Operations

Investing in even a small degree of system flexibility requires changes to business processes, investments in information sharing, and a rethinking of the organizational structure.

For example, a dedicated manufacturing strategy, where each plant is focused on one product family, allows the supply chain to work in a decentralized fashion. Each plant is fully autonomous, and coordination across plants is not required. This is not the case under systems flexibility. Here there is a need to share information about the status, availability, inventories, and backlogs at the various plants so that production and raw materials are allocated to each plant based on system performance.

This is implemented through an important supply chain management process called *sales and operation planning* (S&OP). This is a business process that continuously balances supply and demand. It is cross-functional—integrating sales, marketing, new product launch, manufacturing, and distribution into a single plan, typically at an aggregated volume level, such as product family.

S&OP practice started in the mid-1980s and has focused mainly on demand planning and analysis. The process involves monthly (or quarterly) meetings where demand forecasts and supply capacity constraints are compared and feasible execution plans are identified. Most companies use some demand planning software and spreadsheet analysis of data collected from various enterprise resource planning, customer relationship management, and manufacturing systems.

Here is where system flexibility plays an important role because this is where the company's production sourcing decisions are made. This is unlike a static strategy, where sourcing decisions are updated once a year, distributed to plants and business units, and implemented (or not implemented) at the units' discretion. In a flexible supply chain, companies move from a static sourcing strategy to a dynamic one by optimizing production sourcing decisions, taking into account changes in demand, supply, various costs, and business constraints.

This flexible manufacturing strategy and corresponding S&OP process were implemented at Pepsi Bottling Group (PBG), a large manufacturer and distributor of soft drinks, whose challenges were described in chapter 1. The transformation of the supply chain was remarkable. The journey of PBG started with a six-month proof-of-concept and was followed by implementation across the entire supply chain. Over a period of two years, the firm observed the following changes:[4]

• The creation of regular meetings that brought together supply chain, transportation, finance, sales, and manufacturing functions to discuss sourcing and pre-build strategies,
• A reduction in raw material and supplies inventory from $201 million to $195 million,
• A two percentage point decline in growth of transport miles even as revenue grew, and
• An additional 12.3 million cases available to be sold due to reduction in warehouse out-of-stock levels.

To put this in perspective, the reduction in warehouse out-of-stock effectively added one and a half production lines without requiring any capital expenditure.

7.4 Summary

Achieving flexibility through system design can generate significant returns and provide a deep understanding of the operations trade-offs. The flexibility gained can create a source of competitive advantage by improving along multiple dimensions—operational cost, response time, service levels, and ultimately customer experience. This is the type of transformation that can help management outperform the competition.

Acknowledgment

Many of the ideas covered in this chapter, including the concept of the long chain, were introduced by W. C. Jordan and S. C. Graves.[5]

Notes

1. M. Hammer and J. Champy, *Reengineering the Corporation* (New York: HarperBusiness, 1993).

2. D. Upton, "The Management of Manufacturing Flexibility," *California Management Review* 36 (1994): 72–89.

3. W. C. Jordan and S. C. Graves, "Principles on the Benefits of Manufacturing Process Flexibility," *Management Science* 41, no. 4 (1995): 577–594.

4. D. Simchi-Levi, T. Russell, B. Charles, T. McLoughlin, and P. Hamilton, "Case Study: Transforming Production Sourcing at Pepsi Bottling Group," White paper, IBM and PBG, November 2009.

5. Jordan and Graves, "Principles on the Benefits of Manufacturing Process Flexibility."

8

Process Flexibility

The previous chapter focused on achieving supply chain flexibility through the coordination of activities across the manufacturing and distribution networks. In this chapter, the same concept that was applied for system flexibility is adopted for a single production line, allowing the line to achieve flexibility by focusing on workforce skills and processes.

Achieving flexibility through process design is at the heart of the Toyota production system.[1] These types of production systems are also referred to as *just-in-time* (JIT) or *lean manufacturing*. To put the Toyota Production System in perspective, this chapter starts with a review of the automotive industry.

In the 1970s, the focus of Detroit's big three automotive manufacturing companies was on comfort features such as air conditioning and power steering. The fall of market barriers in the mid-1980s and the accompanying strong performance of Japanese manufacturing companies forced a shift to quality and, in the 1990s, to product variety and flexibility.

The first significant effort to understand Toyota's success story and the automotive industry was an MIT research project whose results are summarized in the 1990 book *The Machine That Changed the World* by J. P. Womack, D. T. Jones, and D. Roos.[2] The book illustrates that in the mid-1980s there was a significant difference between the effectiveness of Toyota's and General Motors' production systems (table 8.1).[3]

The gap between Toyota and the Detroit big three has been shrinking in the last few years, but it still exists. According to the 2008 Harbour Report, "Toyota Motor Corp. and Chrysler LLC led the industry in productivity, with each averaging 30.37 hours to fully assemble a vehicle." By contrast, Chrysler and its Detroit neighbors are behind in profit per vehicle because of the "higher costs for health care, pensions, sales incentives and the higher number of dealerships they support."[4]

Table 8.1
Comparing General Motors and Toyota manufacturing plants, about 1986

	General Motors, Framingham, MA	Toyota, Takaoka
Assembly hours per car	31	16
Assembly defects per 100 cars	130	45
Assembly space per car (square feet per car per year)	8.1	4.8
Inventories of parts (average)	2 weeks	2 hours

Source: J. P. Womack, D. T. Jones, and D. Roos, *The Machine That Changed the World* (New York: HarperPerennial, 1990).

To understand the importance and role that flexibility plays in the Toyota production system, we review its key objectives:[5]

• *Eliminate waste.*   Eliminate all forms of waste including in material, inventory, energy, transportation, defects, time, and cost.

• *Emphasize continuous improvement.*   Constant emphasis is placed on reducing set-ups, improving quality, modifying product design, and adjusting processes.

• *Invest in people and teamwork.*   The manufacturing environment is designed to empower employees to make decisions (such as stopping the production line when a problem is identified), foster problem-solving capability, motivate employees to suggest process improvements, and provide flexibility through worker cross-training.

These objectives complement each other. For example, low work-in-process inventory (waste) implies that there is no fat that masks production line problems. This allows immediate sensing of bottlenecks, line errors, defects, and other manufacturing problems and fosters problem-solving capabilities (people and teamwork). At the same time, production line workers are the best people to propose process improvements, thus continuously enhancing performance and product quality. Similarly, to improve quality and prevent rework (continuous improvement), the Toyota production system advocates "quality at the source." Workers, not inspectors, are responsible for the quality of their work at each stage of the production process (empowering people).

It should be apparent that the lean paradigm is different from the mass-production approach that had prevailed for many years. For instance, in mass production, decisions are made hierarchically, work-in-process inventory is a buffer applied to smooth production, and the environment (set-ups, costs, or quality) is accepted as a constraint that is difficult to improve. By contrast, in a lean production process, decision making is delegated to workers, inventory is considered to be a source of waste that needs to be reduced, and there is a continuous push to remove constraints such as set-ups or quality problems.

If the lean paradigm continuously reduces work-in-process inventory, how can it support a smooth production schedule? This is an important issue since smooth production allows for cost reduction and better utilization of resources. The answer is a relentless focus on flexibility.

Rule 8.1 *The Toyota production system embraces flexibility.*

At first glance, rule 8.1 seems like a contradiction. How can flexibility be achieved in an environment with low inventory, high utilization of resources, and continuous focus on waste reduction? Toyota's answer to this question is a collection of three themes that are frequently found in lean manufacturing: *system*

· Reduce or completely eliminate set-up times and costs,
· Design U-shaped production lines, and
· Invest in worker cross-training.

Consistent with the discussion in this book, flexibility in the Toyota production system focuses on the ability of the production line to respond to change in the following areas:

· Demand volume and mix,
· Variable processing times,
· Equipment breakdown, and
· Unexpected product rework.

In the next three sections, the three themes that collectively define flexibility in the Toyota production system are discussed.

8.1 Set-Up Times and Costs

The benefits of low or reduced set-up times are clear. High set-up times require the line to produce larger lot sizes to take advantage of economies of scale and thus lead to higher inventory levels. This reduces the time available for other products on the same line and prevents the line from switching frequently from one product to another. As a result, when set-up times are high, we typically find dedicated manufacturing facilities, each of which is focused on one product family. In contrast, low or no set-up time reduces inventory and increases production-line flexibility and responsiveness to change. This is exactly the reason many production managers focus on technology and processes to reduce set-up times.

The question of how to reduce set-up times has been answered by various researchers focusing on lean manufacturing. Here is a summary of what is typically recommended, in increasing levels of implementation complexity and difficulty:[6]

· *Identify maintenance and organizational problems* that add set-ups, and eliminate or reduce their impact.
· *Distinguish between internal and external set-ups.* Internal set-ups are performed only when machines are down, while external set-ups can be completed ahead of time while the machine is still running. This implies that it is important to identify external set-ups (since they do not require stopping the machines) and to develop a process to guarantee these set-ups are completed ahead of time or in parallel.
· *Convert internal setups into external setups,* thus reducing the time the machine needs to stop while performing setups.
· *Eliminate adjustments* that are part of the set-up process and typically take a significant amount of time.
· *Modify product design* for set-up reduction.

We have applied some of these ideas in various industries with great success.

Example 8.1

In a U.S.-based automotive manufacturing company, the standard process on the assembly line started when (1) a piston was attached to the (car) engine, (2) the piston was secured, (3) an instruction sheet was scanned into the computer so it could calibrate the gauge, and finally (4) the piston was gauged. Because waiting for the computer to calibrate the gauge is an external set-up and can be done in parallel to other activities, the process was modified. Step 3 of scanning the sheet and calibrating the gauge was completed in parallel with step 2 of securing the piston. This eliminated a few seconds from the process and improved the production line.

Reducing setup times is not only important in manufacturing but also in service operations. Consider for example the remarkable changes happening all around us in health care. Many of these changes are due to implementation of lean philosophy in patient flow, diagnoses processes, and operating rooms. For example, Stockholm's Karolinska Hospital, one of the leading hospitals in Europe, discovered that nonproductive time was very high in the operating rooms. One source of such non-value added time was due to anesthesia for one patient only starting when the operation of the prior patient was done. By adding a staging area at the entrance to the operating room, and by starting anesthesia prior to the completion of the previous patient's operation, the set up time between operations was reduced from sterilization plus anesthesia down to slightly longer than the time for sterilization of the operating room.[7] Applying lean terminology, anesthesia is an external setup time that can be done in parallel to the operating room (machine) still focusing on the current patient and preparing for the next one.

8.2   U-Shaped Production Lines

In a U-shaped production line, machines or processes are arranged around a U-shaped line in the order in which production operations are performed.[8] Workers are trained to perform multiple tasks or processes, and the layout (figure 8.1), facilitates information sharing between workers and increases flexibility. This design allows workers

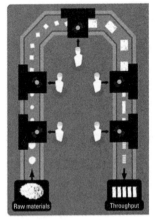

Figure 8.1
A U-shaped production line with no cross-training

to see the various operations and motivates collaboration among workers so that they can adjust production rates and solve problems. As J. Miltenburg observes, "Multi-skilled operators in a U-line comprise a team, and the team becomes the organizational unit accountable for performance."[9]

Typical U-shaped lines operate in a pull mode. Raw materials enter the line only when a finished product is pulled from the line, and the line stops when there is a problem anywhere on the floor. This motivates problem-solving capabilities since the entire unit is responsible for the production line. It also ensures a low level of work-in-process inventory, which in return implies that problems are detected and solved rather quickly.

8.3   Workforce Cross-Training

One important feature in U-shaped lines is worker cross-training—the number and type of tasks that workers should be able to complete in the line. Full-skill cross-training—where each worker can perform all processes—is difficult to achieve and manage and may not be required. On the other hand, no cross-training—where each worker is responsible for only one process—is not appropriate in an environment with process and demand variability and where work in a station can be done in parallel by a number of workers.

There are two main types of *process variability*:

• With *machine variability*, different machines (or stations) on the same line require different processing times for the same piece flowing between the machines
• With *job variability*, different jobs take different lengths of time on the same machine.

Indeed, with machine variability and job variability, one station occasionally will accumulate a significant amount of work that needs to be processed while a neighboring station does not have any and may be waiting for subassemblies. In this situation, cross-training enables multiple workers to share the work in front of loaded stations and thus *reduce processing time*, since they can work in parallel. Having multiple people working at the same station is effective for both processing time and process variability: cross-trained workers sharing work at the same station typically reduce processing time variability at that station.

To demonstrate the effect of cross-training on both processing time and processing time variability, we distinguish between two cases.

Machine Variability

Consider the production line in figure 8.2 with no worker cross-training. The stations (machines) are numbered from 1 (the first station that starts with raw material) to 5 (the last station that produces finished products). Assume that processing time per unit is six minutes on the first, third, and last stations and ten minutes on the second and fourth stations. In this case, the line will produce a finished product every ten minutes, and the line throughput is six units per hour.

The reader may observe that there are two bottlenecks in this production line—one at the second station and another at the fourth station. This is true since these two stations process a subassembly slower than the other stations, leading to starvation of the machines that follow them. That is, the worker responsible for station 3 or station 5 is always idle for four minutes after completing a job in its station. Thus, we say that the line is not *balanced*.

One way to balance the line (and therefore reduce idle time and increase throughput) is to spread the total time for completing a unit (6 + 10 + 6 + 10 + 6 = 38 minutes) equally among the five stations. In this case, the entire processing time on each machine is 38/5 minutes, and the line throughput is thus 7.9 jobs per hour (= 60*5/38). This is the best possible performance for the line, but currently the line throughput is significantly lower (six units per hour).

Unfortunately, redistributing processing times among stations is typically impossible, so it may not be possible to increase the line throughput

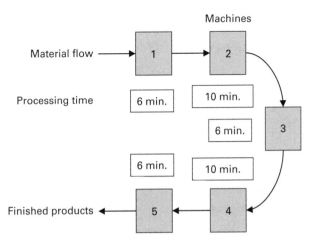

Figure 8.2
A five-station production line with no cross-training

and reduce machine idle time. If workers on the faster stations are cross-trained, however, they can help slower stations during their idle time and hence increase line throughput and machine utilization.

For instance, if the workers assigned to stations 3 and 5 (the fast stations) are cross-trained to do the tasks of stations 2 and 4, respectively, then the following simple policy can be applied. Assume that stations 3 and 5 both have five subassemblies in front of them. A worker at these stations will take thirty minutes to complete these jobs, after which he can switch to a neighboring station (the worker assigned to station 5 switches to station 4, and the one assigned to 3 switches to station 2), process a single job, and switch again to his original station, where another set of five jobs will be ready (the three jobs that were processed by the previous station during the first thirty minutes and the additional two that have been processed in parallel). Thus, in a cycle of forty minutes, the line will produce five finished products, increasing the throughput from six units per hour to 7.5 units per hour.

The problem addressed by cross-training in this example is caused by an unbalanced line—one that has different processing times at different stations. In this case, cross-training balances the line by increasing the throughput of stations 2 and 4 from one product every ten minutes to one job per eight minutes (five jobs every forty minutes).

The only reason the line did not produce at its maximum theoretical throughput (7.9 units per hour) is because the first station is not utilized effectively. By contrast, the other four stations have the same utilization, thus improving line efficiency. This leads to two important rules:

Rule 8.2   *To achieve the maximum line throughput, balance the production line by achieving the same worker utilization.*

Rule 8.3   *Cross-training, properly implemented, equalizes worker utilization.*

Figure 8.3 illustrates three different levels of cross-training and is similar to the supply chain designs depicted in figure 7.1 of chapter 7. The same insight that was developed in the previous chapter applies here: a small investment in flexibility (for instance, two-skill cross-training) will increase throughput and smooth the flow of products on the line.

Rule 8.4   *Small levels of cross-training achieve most of the benefits of full-skill cross-training.*

No cross-training   Two-skill cross-training   Full-skill cross-training

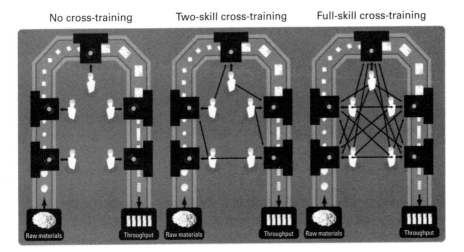

Figure 8.3
Three U-shaped production lines—no cross-training, two-skill cross-training, and full-skill cross-training

Job Variability

Similar insights and rules hold even if all stations have the same average processing times (say, ten minutes per job), but there is some variability in processing time. That is, different jobs on the same machine may have different processing times because of inherent variability. In this case, some stations may accumulate jobs while others are idle, so cross-training allows workers to balance the line.

The effect of variability in job-processing times on line throughput is demonstrated in figure 8.4 (based on a similar figure in W. Hopp and M. Spearman). The horizontal coordinate represents line utilization, and the vertical coordinate represents production cycle time (the inverse of production throughput).[10] The increase in variability implies the following:

· For the same line utilization, production cycle time increases, and hence throughput decreases, and
· For the same cycle time (or throughput), line utilization decreases.

Therefore, similarly to the discussion in chapter 7,[11]

Rule 8.5   *Variability degrades production-line performance.*

Going back to the production line shown in figure 8.2, we tested the effect of job and machine variability on line performance with and

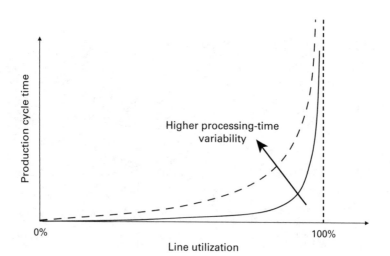

Figure 8.4
Production cycle time and line utilization as functions of processing-time variability

without worker cross-training. In these experiments, we kept each station's average processing time according to the information in figure 8.2, and we increased job variability on each machine. The results are summarized in figures 8.5 and 8.6.

As is shown in figure 8.5, two-skill cross-training significantly decreased the average time between releases of a new finished product, or equivalently it significantly increased the line throughput. Similarly, two-skill cross-training magically decreased the average work-in-process inventory, as is illustrated by figure 8.6.

To fully appreciate the impact of cross-training, we also analyzed the same production line with the added constraint of limiting work-in-process inventory in front of each machine. The figures illustrate that two-skill cross-training with limited buffer inventory provided the same throughput as without limiting buffer inventory but significantly lowered work in process inventory (see figures 8.5 and 8.6).

In 2008, Lamborghini, the Italian manufacturer of luxury and exotic cars implemented lean in its assembly operations. The assembly line for Lamborghini Gallardo consists of 24 stations and includes 40 operators. Cars are produced to order with up to six months from order to delivery—thus it was important to reduce cycle time and increase throughput. The lean implementation, following many of the principles described in this chapter, had a dramatic effect on line performance with 40 percent

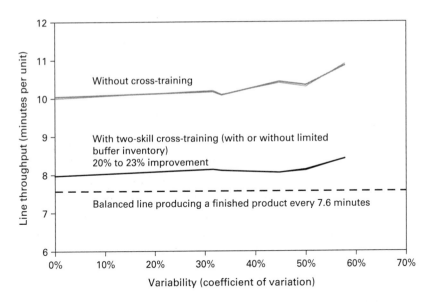

Figure 8.5
Line throughput (minutes per unit) as a function of variability

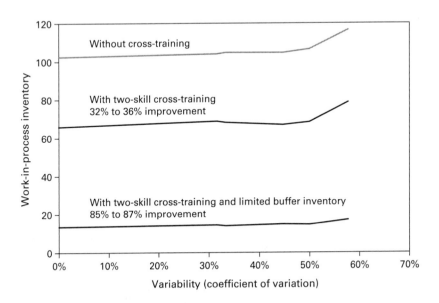

Figure 8.6
Average work-in-process inventory as a function of variability

reduction in production cycle time; increase in throughput from 7 to 11 cars per day; and inventory reduction by a staggering 50 percent.

8.4   Summary

Process flexibility is at the heart of the Toyota production system, which is also called *lean manufacturing* or *just-in-time inventory*. Here flexibility is achieved through worker cross-training that allows the production line to equalize workforce utilization and improve line performance. Much like system flexibility, a small investment in worker cross-training achieves almost all the benefits of full-skill cross-training.

It is appropriate to point out that although this book is about manufacturing, retail, and distribution, lean principles in general and process flexibility in particular can be applied in the service industry as well. Processing bills in banks, processing claims at insurance companies, processing patients in a hospital, or software development projects are all examples of where lean principles can help (service) organizations gain efficiency and reduce costs. Indeed, the importance of setup time reduction, the effects of variability, the need to equalize worker utilization, and the focus on (a small investment in) cross-training are all universal principles and rules that should be followed in the service industry.

Acknowledgment

The ideas in section 8.3 are loosely based on the work of S. M. R. Iravani.[12]

Notes

1. J. Liker, *The Toyota Way* (New York: McGraw-Hill, 1994); W. Hopp and M. Spearman, *Factory Physics*, 2nd ed. (New York: McGraw-Hill, 2000).

2. J. P. Womack, D. T. Jones, and D. Roos, *The Machine That Changed the World* (New York: HarperPerennial, 1990).

3. Ibid.

4. Oliver Wyman, "The Harbour Report, North America," 2008, available at http://www.oliverwyman.com (accessed on March 24, 2010).

5. Liker, *The Toyota Way*.

6. Lean Manufacturing Strategy, available at http://www.strategosinc.com.

7. J. Teboul and J. Tabet, "Karolinska Sjukhuset," 1995, INSEAD case 695-008-1, available at www.ecch.com; Chick S. private communication.

8. J. Miltenburg, "U-shaped Production Lines: A Review of Theory and Practice," *International Journal of Production Economics* 70 (2001): 201–214.

9. Ibid.

10. Hopp and Spearman, *Factory Physics*.

11. Ibid.

12. S. M. R. Iravani, "Design and Control Principles of Flexible Workforce in Manufacturing Systems," *Encyclopedia of Operations Research* (New York: Wiley, forthcoming).

9

Product Design Flexibility

One of the most effective tools for achieving flexibility is product design. Product design is part of the *development chain*—the collection of activities and processes that are associated with the introduction of a new product. It includes the product design phase, the associated capabilities and knowledge that need to be developed internally, sourcing decisions, and production plans. Specifically, the development chain includes decisions about product architecture, make or buy decisions (what to make internally and what to buy from outside suppliers), supplier selection, early supplier involvement, and strategic partnerships.

The development chain and the supply chain intersect at the production point (figure 9.1). This implies that the characteristics of and decisions made in the development chain will affect the supply chain. Similarly, the characteristics of the supply chain must affect product design strategy and hence the development chain.

For example, the framework suggests that decisions made in the development chain (particularly product design decisions) must take into account the effects of these decisions on product life-cycle costs including end-of-life costs. This is supported by data—over 70 percent of product life-cycle costs are locked in at the product design stage.[1]

Thus, at the product design stage, managers need to take a *holistic approach* and evaluate product architecture based on not only material and labor costs but also product life-cycle costs—including inventory implications, packaging, utilization of transportation capacity, impact on the environment, recycling, and material waste.

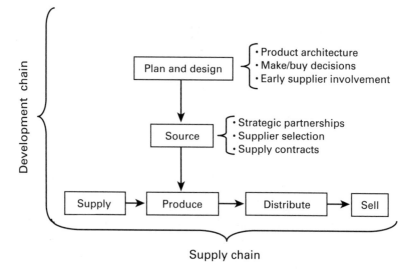

Figure 9.1
The development chain and the supply chain

Example 9.1

Hewlett-Packard was one of the first firms to recognize that development and supply chains intersect. A case in point is HP's introduction of a new generation of network laser printer in the early 1990s. The question was whether to use a universal power supply for the new product, even though earlier generations of the printer used a dedicated power supply (and associated components)—one for the North American market and one for the European market. HP took a holistic approach and analyzed the ways that different product architectures affected not only labor and material costs but also inventory costs during the product life cycle—from ramp-up through maturity all the way to end of life. More recently, HP has focused on making design decisions such as determining design activities that can be outsourced and identifying the corresponding organizational structures needed to manage the outsourced design process by considering the characteristics of both the development and supply chains.[2]

Unfortunately, in most organizations, different managers are responsible for the different activities that are part of these (development and supply) chains. Typically, the vice president of engineering is responsible for the development chain, the VP of manufacturing for the production portion of the chains, and the VP of supply chain or logistics for the fulfillment of customer demand. These managers usually have performance incentives that focus on their individual responsibilities, often ignoring the effects of their decisions on the other portion of the development and supply chains. Unless carefully addressed, these organizational and incentive structures typically result in a misalignment of product design and supply chain strategies.

9.1 Development Chain Characteristics

Each chain has different characteristics. For example, key characteristics of the supply chain include the following:

· Demand uncertainty and variability,
· Economies of scale in production and transportation, and
· Lead time, particularly because of globalization.

Each of these dimensions significantly affects the appropriate supply chain strategy—see chapter 3 for a framework that matches these dimensions with supply chain strategies.

The development chain provides a different set of challenges. It can be characterized by the following:

· *Innovation speed*   The speed by which technology changes in a particular industry. This affects product design and hence the development chain.
· *Make/buy decisions*   Decisions regarding what to make internally and what to buy from outside suppliers. These decisions are determined, in part, based on internal (development chain) capabilities and (supply chain) capacities.
· *Product structure*   The level of modularity or integrality of a product. The concept of modularity in product architecture is discussed in more detail later in this chapter, but for the purposes of this section, it is sufficient to say that a highly modular product is assembled from a variety of modules and that each module can have several options. By contrast, an integral product is made up from components whose functionalities are tightly related and whose design is closely integrated. Integral products are evaluated based on system performance, not based on component performance.

Of course, in the real world, very few products are either modular or integral. Indeed, the degree of modularity or integrality varies with desktop computers on one end of the spectrum (highly modular products), and the iPhone on the other end (highly integral product). A car is a product that includes many modular components (the stereo system or other electronic systems) and many integral components (for example, the engine).

Concepts such as the development chain and innovation speed are directly related to the two product types, innovative products and functional products (discussed in previous chapters). *Functional products* are characterized by slow innovation speed, low product variety, and typically low profit margins. Examples include grocery products such as soup, beer, tires, and office equipment. *Innovative products* are characterized by fast technology clock-speed, short product life cycle, high product variety, and relatively high margins. Examples include cell phones, personal computers, printers, fashion items and cosmetics.

9.2   Matching Strategies with Chain Characteristics

The supply chain strategy that the firm must use for innovative products is quite different from the one that is appropriate for functional products (see section 3.5 in chapter 3). Indeed, both the supply chain strategy and the degree of flexibility for a fast clock-speed product (such as PCs or laser printers) are quite different from the supply chain strategy and the level of supply chain flexibility for a slow clock-speed product (such as diapers and tires).

So *what is the appropriate product design strategy for each product type?* Clearly, products with fast innovation speed require a different approach than products with slow innovation speed. Similarly, product design strategy depends on the characteristics of the supply chain. Therefore, we need a framework that takes both aspects—innovation speed and supply chain characteristics—into account.

Figure 9.2 provides a framework for matching product design and supply chain strategies with the characteristics of the development chain (innovation speed) and the supply chain (demand uncertainty). The horizontal axis provides information on demand uncertainty while the vertical axis represents product introduction frequency (or product innovation speed).

Everything else being equal, higher demand uncertainty leads to a preference for managing the supply chain based on a pull strategy (see chapter 3). Alternatively, smaller demand uncertainty leads to an interest in managing the supply chain using a push strategy. In a push strategy, the focus is on having predictable demand, leveraging high economies of scale, and achieving cost efficiencies. In a pull supply chain, the focus is

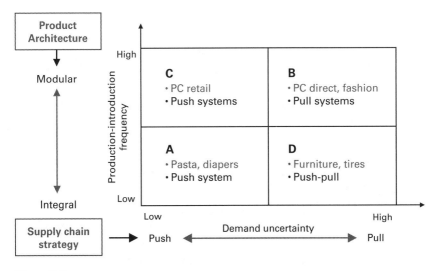

Figure 9.2
The effects of demand uncertainty and product introduction frequency on product design and supply chain strategies

on reacting to unpredictable demand, dealing with low economies of scale, and achieving flexibility and responsiveness.

Similarly, everything else being equal, high product introduction frequency (fast innovation speed) suggests a focus on *modular product architecture*. This allows the independent development of product sub-components. The final selection of features and product differentiation are postponed as much as possible—sometimes until demand is realized. Such an architecture also allows reusing various components (such as PC monitors) when the technology of others (such as CPU) have changed so that they need to be replaced.

For all its benefits (the flexibility to match products with customer requirements), modularity comes with significant side effects. Developing a modular product architecture requires significantly more time than an integral product, is more difficult to accomplish, is more expensive, and can negatively affect quality and performance. This is true since in a modular architecture, there are many combinations that may not be fully compatible, and hence the design may be slightly compromised compared to the optimal integral design. So modularity should be pursued cautiously.

Thus, an integral product architecture is recommended when product introduction frequency is low (for slow innovation speed). Such a design is typically simpler, easier to implement, and often less expensive.

In figure 9.2, the region spanned by these two dimensions—demand uncertainty and product introduction frequency—is partitioned into four boxes. Box A represents products that are characterized by predictable demand and slow product introduction frequency. Examples include products like diapers, soup, and pasta. The framework suggests that these products should focus on a push strategy, supply chain efficiency, and high inventory turns. Product modularity is less important.

Box B represents products with fast innovation speed and highly unpredictable demand. Many high-tech products (such as PCs sold directly over the Internet, printers, and cell phones) and fashion items belong to this category. Here the focus is on flexibility and responsiveness, on pull strategy, and on modular product architecture. Thus, products in this category require a supply chain that values responsiveness over cost.

Box D represents products with slow innovation speed but high demand uncertainty. These are the products and industries where a combination of push and pull is essential. Similarly to box B, these are also situations where lead time reduction, if possible, is important. Examples of products in this category include high-end furniture, chemical products such as agrochemicals, commodity chemicals, and specialty chemicals, and products such as large diameter tires used in the mining industry where volume is relatively small and so demand is highly unpredictable.

In this case, the push-pull implementation depends on the characteristics of the specific industry. For instance, chemical products are characterized by a complex production process with multiple recipes (this corresponds to a bill of material in discrete manufacturing) and long lead times, so here push-pull is implemented by positioning buffer inventory in key manufacturing stages. This is not the case for high-end furniture manufacturing companies where assembly is to order (pull) and distribution is based on a fixed schedule (push).

Finally, box C represents products with fast innovation speed and low demand uncertainty. These innovative products (such as PCs, cell phones, and printers) are sold through retail chains. This is a unique case, where the supply chain strategy is push (focusing on cost reduction), but product design strategy is focused on modular product architecture to achieve *flexibility in response to changes in technology*. This is appropriate, since high product introduction frequency does not necessarily imply that all product modules are obsolete but rather that new technology will replace some of the existing modules. Thus, a modular architecture is required.

Push is appropriate since demand uncertainty is low and the focus is on efficiency or cost reduction.

To summarize, the need to respond to changes in demand and technology (box B) or just a change in technology (box C) require flexibility and hence a modular product architecture.

Rule 9.1 *Modular product architecture is important when flexibility is required.*

The framework presented here is also helpful in evaluating Nokia versus Apple cell phone design and supply chain strategies. Apple's cell phone division has a single product, the iPhone, compared with hundreds of different phones and configurations for Nokia. Similarly, Nokia's product introduction frequency is higher than that of Apple. Thus, Nokia is in box B (when selling its products online) or box C (retail) and therefore must apply a modular product architecture. In contrast, Apple's iPhone characteristics match that of box A and hence require an integral product architecture.

Modular product architecture requires standardization, both of parts and processes.[3] In *part standardization*, common parts are used across many products. Common parts reduce the level of demand uncertainty and hence part inventories due to risk pooling (see rule 3.1). They also reduce part costs through economies of scale. Of course, excessive part commonality can reduce product differentiation, so that less expensive customization options might cannibalize sales of more expensive parts.

Process standardization involves standardizing as much of the process as possible for different products and then customizing the products as late as possible. In this case, products and manufacturing processes are designed so that decisions about which specific product is manufactured—differentiation—can be delayed until after manufacturing is under way. The manufacturing process starts by making a *generic* or *family* product that is later differentiated into a specific end product. For this reason, this approach is also known as *postponement* or *delayed product differentiation*.[4] By delaying differentiation, production can be based on aggregate forecasts. Thus, design for delayed product differentiation can be effectively used to address the uncertainty in customer demand even if forecasts cannot be improved.

It is usually necessary to redesign products specifically for delayed differentiation. For example, it may be required to resequence the manufacturing process to take advantage of process standardization.

Resequencing refers to modifying the order of product manufacturing steps so that the operations that result in the differentiation of specific items or products are postponed as much as possible. One famous and dramatic example of a firm that utilized resequencing to improve its supply chain operation is Benetton Corporation.

Example 9.2

Benetton is a major supplier of knitwear, Europe's largest clothing manufacturer, and the world's largest consumer of wool in the garment sector.[5] It supplies thousands of stores all over the world. The nature of the fashion industry is that consumer preferences change rapidly. Because of Benetton's long manufacturing lead time, store owners frequently had to place orders for wool sweaters up to seven months before the sweaters would appear in their stores. The wool sweater manufacturing process typically consists of acquiring yarn, dyeing it, finishing it, manufacturing the garment parts, and then joining those parts into a completed sweater. This process allowed little flexibility in responding to the changing tastes of consumers. To address this issue, Benetton revised its manufacturing process, postponing the dyeing of the garments until after the sweater was completely assembled so that color choices could be delayed until after more forecasting and sales information could be received. By postponing the dyeing process, yarn purchasing and manufacturing plans could be based on aggregate forecasts for product families rather than forecasts for specific sweater and color combinations. This revised process made sweater manufacturing about 10 percent more expensive and required the purchasing of new equipment and the retraining of employees. However, Benetton was more than adequately compensated by improved forecasts, lower surplus inventories, and, in many cases, higher sales.[6]

A U.S. disk drive manufacturer provides another notable example. In this example, lower levels of inventory need to be held in order to achieve specific service levels, but the per unit inventory cost tends to be more expensive.

Example 9.3

A major U.S. manufacturer of mass storage devices makes unique hard-drive products for various customers. Orders are placed to be delivered by a certain time, and since lead times are long, the manufacturer has to keep a variety of products in process to meet promised delivery dates. Since variability of demand is high and each product is unique, the

Example 9.3
(continued)

manufacturer has to maintain high levels of in-process inventory to meet demand reliably. The manufacturing process involves a brief generic segment, through which products intended for all customers must go, and then an extensive customization portion. The ideal point to hold inventory is before customization begins. Unfortunately, because of time-consuming testing, most manufacturing time occurs after differentiation has started. This testing has to take place after differentiation starts because a particular circuit board has to be added to the assembly for the testing to take place, and this circuit board is different for each customer. To delay differentiation, a generic circuit board can be inserted into the assembly so that much of the testing can be completed. The generic circuit board can be removed, and the customer-specific boards can be added later. In this way, disk drive differentiation can be delayed until more order information is available. This process decreases the level of required in-process inventory needed to meet demand reliably, but it adds some additional manufacturing steps (adding and removing the generic board). Thus, it is necessary to compare the manufacturing inefficiencies caused by adding and removing this circuit board with the gains in inventory savings. The manufacturing processes are illustrated in figure 9.3.[7]

Part standardization and process standardization are frequently connected. Sometimes part standardization is necessary for implementing process standardization.

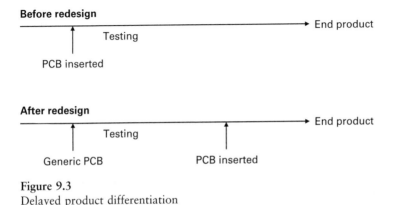

Figure 9.3
Delayed product differentiation

Example 9.4

A major printer manufacturer was preparing to introduce a new color printer into the market. Demand for the new printer and an existing printer was expected to be highly variable and negatively correlated. The manufacturing processes for the two products were similar, except that different circuit boards and print-head assemblies were used. Differences in head assemblies and circuit boards led to very different manufacturing processes. To implement process standardization (delayed differentiation), the manufacturing processes need to be similar until the final step. To do this, the printers have been redesigned so that both products share a common circuit board and print head. This ensures that differentiation can be delayed as much as possible. Thus, in this case, part standardization enables process standardization.[8]

In some cases, resequencing and part commonality allow the final manufacturing steps to be completed at distribution centers or warehouses instead of at the factory and hence achieve a higher level of flexibility. This is true since distribution centers typically are much closer to market demand than the factories, and hence products can be differentiated closer to the demand, increasing the firm's ability to respond to rapidly changing markets.

Sometimes, processes can be redesigned so that the differentiating steps do not have to be performed in a manufacturing facility or distribution center but can take place at the retailer's after the sale is made. Often this is accomplished by focusing on modularity during the design phase, placing functionality in *modules* that can be easily added to a product. For example, many laser printers and copiers are packaged in their most basic version. Along with the printer, each retail store stocks separately packaged modules that add features (such as advanced paper handling or stapling) to the printer or copier. This strategy can greatly lower required inventory since only extended features can be stocked in module form, instead of entire printers.

9.3   Summary

In some industries such as high-tech, fashion, and chemicals, product design is an essential enabler of flexibility. Modular product architecture, postponement, standard processes and common parts provide manufacturing flexibility and allow the supply chain to respond to changes in technology, demand mix, and volume.

→ tradeoffs

But product modularity comes with all sorts of complications—longer development time, increased complexity and costs, performance and quality challenges, and a need for a higher degree of coordination. Thus, modularity is not a silver bullet. What is needed is a holistic view at the product design stage that enables managers to evaluate various design alternatives based not only on labor and material costs but also on product life-cycle costs.

This will become even more apparent in the next two chapters, which analyze the effects of escalating oil prices and corporate social responsibility.

Notes

1. J. Corbett, "Design for eWonomic Manufacture," *CIRP* 35, no. 1 (1986): 93–97.

2. H. L. Lee, "Hewlett-Packard Company: Network Printer Design for Universality," Stanford Global Supply Chain Management Forum Case Study, Stanford University, 1996.

3. J. M. Swaminathan, "Enabling Customization Using Standardized Operations," *California Management Review* 43, no. 3 (2001): 125–135.

4. H. L. Lee, "Design for Supply Chain Management: Concepts and Examples," Working paper, Department of Industrial Engineering and Engineering Management, Stanford University, 1992.

5. "Fashion Houses: Benetton," available at http://www.made-in-italy.com (accessed on December 23, 2009).

6. S. Signorelli and J. Heskett, "Benetton (A)," *Harvard University Business School Case,* Case no. 9-685-014, 1984.

7. Lee, "Design for Supply Chain Management."

8. Ibid.

III

Emerging Trends

10

The Effects of Oil Price Volatility

In the summer of 2008, oil prices reached a peak of $145 per barrel, and analysts and pundits predicted that they will continue to rise. As the recession hit the global economy, oil prices reversed and plunged to $33 per barrel. By late 2009, oil prices were fluctuating wildly, and the trend is now upward. For example, oil prices had increased by almost 90 percent between January 2009 and January 2010.

Of course, the level of volatility in oil price has a large impact on supply chain strategies. Specifically, with rising and volatile oil prices, classical strategies such as just-in-time inventory, lean manufacturing, off-shoring, or frequent deliveries to retail outlets might drive up costs and imperil the supply chain.

Given this volatility in oil prices and its potential effects on the supply chain, a firm may consider one of two options for its transportation strategy, with each carrying a significant risk. The first is to focus on long-term, or forward, contracts to hedge against oil price volatility. Unfortunately, such contracts can be too expensive if oil prices move in the wrong direction. The second possible strategy is to rely on spot purchasing, but this exposes the firm to both price and shortage risks. More importantly, if many companies follow such a short-term reactive strategy, oil price volatility is likely to increase. So how should smart executives cope with rising and volatile oil prices?

In this chapter, we answer the question by exploring the relationship between oil price and supply chain strategies.

10.1   Oil Prices and Logistics Costs

The annual *State of Logistics Report*, sponsored by the Council of Supply Chain Management Professionals and first published in 1989, provides an accounting of the nation's total logistics costs and tracks

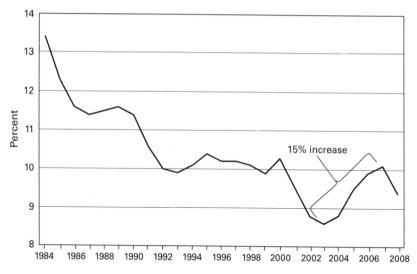

Figure 10.1
Logistics costs as a percentage of the U.S. economy

trends in transportation costs, inventory-carrying costs, and total logistics costs.

As is shown in figure 10.1, U.S. logistics costs were over 12 percent of gross domestic product in the early 1980s and steadily decreased until 2003. The numbers are staggering: in 1998 the amount was $884 billion, and in 2007 it was $1.4 trillion, $49 billion higher than logistics costs in 2008. The decrease in 2008 logistics costs is attributed mostly to a decrease in inventory costs. Inventory carrying costs decreased 13 percent between 2007 and 2008, mostly due to a decrease in inventory carrying rate of about 11 percent and a decrease in actual inventory of 2 percent. Transportation costs stayed more or less flat.

In contrast, between 2002 and 2007, U.S. logistics costs increased by more than 50 percent. According to the *State of Logistics Report*, the increase was driven by "high fuel costs, truck driver and rail capacity shortages, off-shoring and outsourcing and the costs of security."

The various cost components that constitute U.S. logistics costs are presented in figure 10.2, taken again from the *State of Logistics Report*. Transportation cost is by far the largest cost component, and inventory cost is slightly higher than half of the transportation costs.

The increases in transportation costs between 2002 and 2007 are well understood. High energy costs, limited rail capacity, shortage of truck drivers, and tighter security requirements have all contributed to increased transportation costs. But why did inventory levels and costs

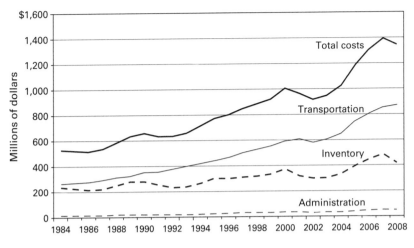

Figure 10.2
Total U.S. logistics costs, 1984 to 2008

increase significantly during that period? Some reasons include long lead times due to off-shoring, more products competing in the same market, and demanding retailers and customers that require a higher level of service.

You might be surprised, but high transportation costs also lead to higher inventory. This is true since as transportation costs increase, shippers try to reduce costs by shipping large quantities and taking advantage of economies of scale. Unfortunately, this action contributes to higher inventory levels. Thus, a direct relationship exists between energy costs, transportation costs, and higher levels of inventory.

10.2 Expensive Fuel for Thought

Changes in oil prices affect transportation surcharges for various modes of transportation. To understand the relationship between the two, figure 10.3 depicts average U.S. diesel price at the pump and crude oil price (in cents per gallon) from 1999 to 2010. Not surprisingly, both diesel prices and crude oil prices move in parallel. A more detailed analysis suggests that in the United States, a $10 per barrel increase in crude oil price produces a twenty-four-cent-per-gallon increase in diesel fuel.[1] Since the standard methodology applied by carriers is to increase transportation surcharges by one cent per mile for every six-cent increase in diesel fuel, a $10 increase for a barrel of crude oil produces a four-cent-per-mile increase in transportation rates.

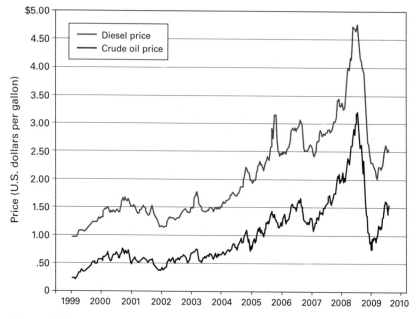

Figure 10.3
U.S. diesel and crude oil prices, 1999 to 2010

Table 10.1
Truckload carrier sensitivity to oil price

Crude oil (U.S. dollars per barrel)	$75	$100	$125	$150	$175	$200
Truckload (U.S. dollars per mile)	$1.65	$1.75	$1.85	$1.95	$2.05	$2.15
Increase (percent)	0	6%	12%	18%	24%	30%

Table 10.1 shows how these figures affect a typical truck-load (TL) transportation rate. For example, as crude oil price increases from $75 per barrel to $150 per barrel, truck-load rate per mile will increase by about 18 percent.

The same analysis was conducted with data from Belgium, Germany, Italy, the Netherlands, and the United Kingdom. Here, a $10 per barrel increase in crude oil price will result in between twelve to fifteen cents (€0.076 to € 0.094) per liter increase in diesel fuel depending on the country. So a $10 increase for a barrel of crude oil could produce a seven-to-nine-cent-per-mile increase in transportation rates depending on the country (based on the assumption of approximately 4.5 kilometer per liter of fuel consumption). This suggests that these European countries are more vulnerable to changes in crude oil prices than the United States.

10.3 Impact on the Logistics Network

Since the mid-1990s, many corporations have tried to reduce operational costs and achieve a lean supply chain by emphasizing manufacturing outsourcing, off-shoring, plant rationalization, and facility consolidation. The underlying rationale behind these trends was cheap oil. Indeed, in many industries transportation costs accounted for just a few percentage points of total operational costs. Hence, more emphasis was given to reducing manufacturing costs through off-shoring or outsourcing, rationalizing plants to take advantage of economies of scale in production costs and reduce capital investment, and consolidating distribution centers and warehouses to reduce inventory levels and fixed facility costs.

The recent increases in oil price are starting to reverse this trend. Indeed, as crude oil prices increase, transportation costs become more important relative to inventory, production, and facility fixed costs. Thus, three trade-offs emerge:

Regional distribution centers are more attractive.   As oil prices increase, outbound transportation costs become more expensive, and as a consequence it is increasingly more important to minimize the distance of the final leg—from distribution centers to retail outlets. This can be achieved by establishing more warehouses, each responsible for a specific region. Of course, more warehouses imply more safety stock and hence higher inventory levels. Finally, as explained in section 10.1, the increase in transportation costs will force companies to ship large quantities to take advantage of economies of scale. Therefore, larger warehouses will be needed.

Example 10.1[2]

A U.S.-based company has manufacturing facilities in Philadelphia, Omaha, and Juarez, Mexico. The Juarez facility is the lowest-cost operation. The company has five distribution centers that serve demand in the U.S. Facing rising fuel prices, it undertook a network design study to accomplish the following:

Example 10.1
(continued)

· *Identify the right number and location of distribution centers and appropriate assignment of customers to DCs,*
· *Determine the best allocation of products across the company's manufacturing and distribution facilities, and*
· *Understand how the network should change as oil prices fluctuate.*

The study revealed a significant need to reduce outbound transportation costs by utilizing more distribution centers that stock more inventory; see figure 10.4. The figure shows that the number of distribution centers increases from five to seven as oil costs rise from $75 to $200 per barrel.

Sourcing and production move closer to demand. As cheaper manufacturing costs (frequently associated with off-shoring) are offset by higher transportation costs, more and more manufacturing and sourcing activities will move to near-shoring. This is nicely illustrated by total landed costs which include unit costs, transportation costs, inventory and handling costs, duties and taxation, and the costs of finance. Landed cost represents the effective cost of sourcing or manufacturing in one location and serving customers in other locations and should be used when evaluating sourcing and manufacturing decisions. Evidently, as transportation costs increase, the role of sourcing and production costs in total landed cost diminishes.

Example 10.2

Consider again the previous example. The study also showed that as oil prices increase, so does the need for production to move closer to demand. In this case, the advantages of cheaper manufacturing in Mexico are offset by higher transportation costs (figure 10.5).

The need to move manufacturing facilities from low cost countries to near market demand in the United States is exacerbated by financial pressure to reduce time to market. These two forces—the effect of transportation on total landed costs and the pressure to reduce time to market—motivate some industries to move manufacturing facilities from Asia to Mexico, as is illustrated by the next example.

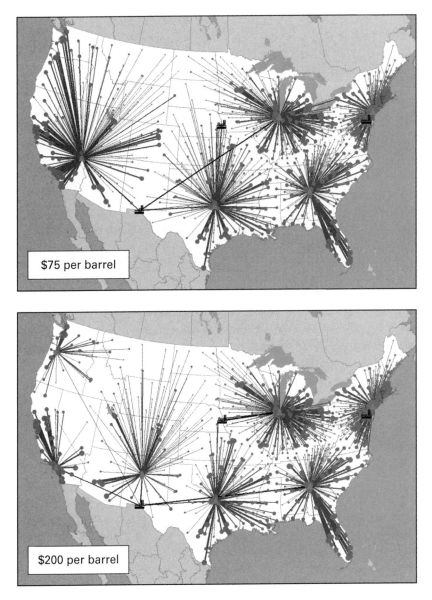

Figure 10.4
Reducing transportation costs by increasing the number of regional distribution centers. As costs per barrel rise from $75 to $200, the optimal number of DCs increases from five to seven, and Las Vegas is replaced by Los Angeles, Albuquerque, and Portland.

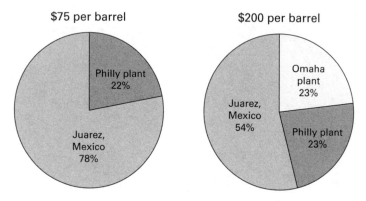

Figure 10.5
Reducing transportation costs by locating manufacturing plants near markets

Example 10.3

The TV manufacturer Sharp has recently started moving manufacturing facilities from Asia to Mexico to serve customers in North and South America. This move is driven by the need to keep shipping costs low and time to market short. Indeed, prices of televisions typically fall fast, so reducing shipping time from about forty days (when flat TVs were produced in Asia) to seven days significantly improves the bottom line.[3]

Supply chain flexibility becomes the focus of the organization. As oil price and volatility increase, it becomes more important to serve demand from the closest manufacturing plant. However, this is not possible if each plant specializes in producing just a few products, a strategy known as dedicated manufacturing (see chapter 7). A dedicated manufacturing environment often reduces manufacturing costs because economies of scale come into play and fewer set-ups are required to switch between different products. Unfortunately, such a strategy may result in long delivery legs to market demand and hence higher transportation costs. By contrast, a full flexibility manufacturing strategy, where each plant is able to produce all (or almost all) products, increases production costs (due to frequent set-ups and smaller lot sizes) but reduces transportation costs.

The implications are clear! The higher the price of a barrel of oil, the more important it is to invest in a flexible strategy because it reduces transportation costs. This is illustrated in example 10.4, which shows that a small investment in a flexible manufacturing strategy reduces the increase in supply chain costs from 14 percent for the dedicated strategy to 3.5 percent for the flexible one, as oil price increases from $100 per barrel to $200 per barrel.

Example 10.4[4]

A European manufacturing company has five plants located in Geel, Belgium; Hamburg, Germany; Lecce, Italy; Pordenone, Italy; and Cheltenham, UK. Each facility is dedicated to a single product family. Inbound transportation uses large trucks (15,000 kilograms per shipment), while outbound transportation deploys smaller trucks (5,000 kg/shipment). As figure 10.6 illustrates, when each plant is dedicated to a single product family and the structure of the logistics network is optimized, an increase in crude oil price from $100 per barrel to $200 per barrel will increase supply chain costs by 14 percent, even if the firm adjusts the distribution network by adding four distribution centers.

Not surprisingly, investing in manufacturing flexibility by allowing products to be made at new plants (even when including the investment associated with plant reconfiguration) significantly reduces the increase in supply chain costs from 14 to 3.5 percent (figure 10.7). Interestingly, flexibility is achieved by adding only four new production lines to the existing plants.

The previous example illustrates a recurring theme in this book:

Rule 10.1   *A small investment in system flexibility can help a firm reduce the effects of oil price increases or oil price volatility.*

10.4   Impact on Transportation

Many current transportation strategies, including just-in-time delivery, quick and frequent shipments, and using a dedicated fleet, are based on cheap oil prices. For example, transportation strategies such as quick and frequent deliveries were designed to reduce inventory levels by decreasing lead times and increasing the frequency of deliveries. As oil price increased in 2008, transportation became more expensive relative to inventory, and as a result three important trends emerged:

From just-in-time delivery to better use of transportation capacity.   With this trend, larger lot sizes are shipped less frequently, and efficient packaging is used to improve truckload utilization.

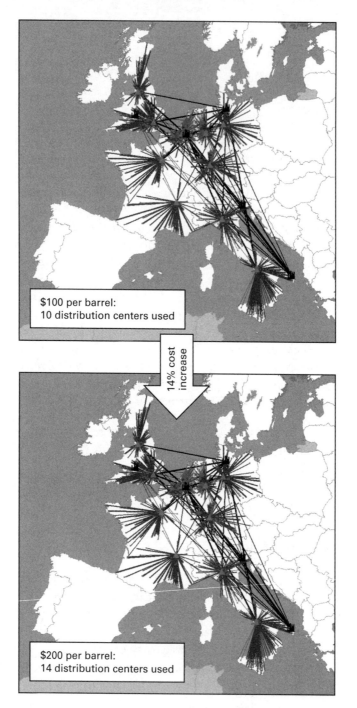

$100 per barrel:
10 distribution centers used

14% cost increase

$200 per barrel:
14 distribution centers used

Figure 10.6
The effect of optimizing the distribution network while keeping a dedicated manufacturing strategy

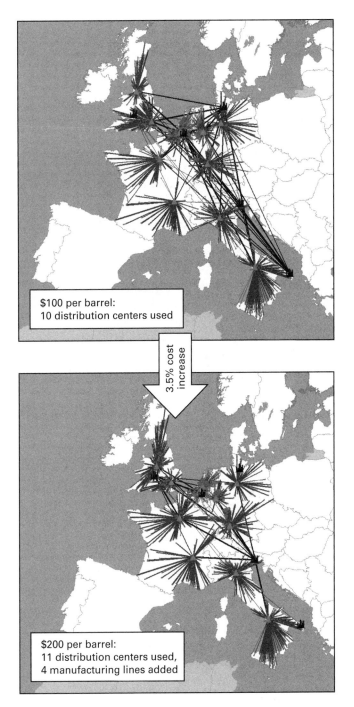

Figure 10.7
Reducing the increase in transportation costs through a flexible manufacturing strategy

Example 10.5

In 2007, S. C. Johnson's truck utilization project saved the firm "$1.6 million and cut fuel use by 168,000 gallons." For example, the firm found that mixing loads of Windex glass cleaner and Ziploc bags, which used to be packed in separate loads, improved its use of truck capacity.[5]

From quick delivery to cheaper and sometimes slower transportation modes. As oil prices increase, more shipments will move from air to ground and from trucking to rail to cut fuel consumption and reduce transportation costs.

From dedicated resources to shared resources. In the new economy of highly volatile oil prices, the role played by shared resources—such as third-party logistics carriers and consolidated warehouses—will increase. Common carriers can consolidate shipments from many vendors and replace less than full truckloads with full truckload shipments. They are also in a better position to reduce deadhead travel, a source of transportation inefficiency. Similarly, large consolidated warehouses aggregate order quantities into full-truckload shipments and reduce total shipping costs.

Example 10.6

Multiple manufacturers store their products in ES3's giant warehouse in York, Pennsylvania, where truckloads are built and shipped to retailers' distribution centers. According to ES3, an important benefit of the consolidated warehouse is reduction in transportation costs.[6]

10.5   Supply Chain Strategies

Beyond their effect on network and transportation strategies, escalating and volatile oil prices affect business strategies in general and supply chains in particular. We start by reviewing important impacts.

More inventory. The analysis in section 10.3 above suggests that higher oil prices will have two important effects—increasing total safety stock in the supply chain (because of the need for more regional warehouses) and increasing lot sizes (to take advantage of economies of scale). At the same time, the switch from quick and frequent deliveries to efficient, slow, and less frequent shipments will also drive up inventory. Thus, assuming that lead times remain the same and that there is no change in sourcing locations, supply chain inventory will increase as oil prices increase.

More push strategies.   Today's supply chain strategies are often categorized as push, pull, or push-pull strategies (see chapter 3). The appropriate supply chain strategy for a particular product depends on a variety
of drivers, but the most important for this discussion is economies of
scale. Everything else being equal, the higher the importance of economies of scale in reducing cost, the greater the value of aggregating
demand and thus the greater the importance of managing the supply
chain based on a long-term forecast—a push-based strategy. As oil prices
increase, the importance of economies of scale (such as shipping large
quantities) increases and hence the importance of a push-based strategy.
Therefore, we expect that escalating oil prices will drive more supply
chain stages toward a push strategy.

Of course, more inventories and a higher degree of push may not be
appropriate in many industries. Thus, executives need to consider mitigation strategies:

Position inventory effectively.   As oil prices increase, trade-offs between
inventory and transportation costs become more important and as a
result positioning inventory correctly can have a dramatic impact on
logistics costs. For example, in a hub-and-spoke network, items are
shipped from manufacturing facilities to primary warehouses (hubs) and
from there to secondary warehouses (spokes) and finally to retail stores.
In such a network, high-volume-low-variability products must be positioned at the secondary warehouses because of the need to take advantage
of economies of scale in transportation costs—safety stock is not an issue
since forecasts are accurate for products with these characteristics. By
contrast, forecast accuracy is poor for low-volume-high-variability products, thus these products are positioned at primary warehouses to reduce
inventory by taking advantage of the risk pooling concept (rule 3.1).

My experience is that many companies are not very good at positioning
inventory in their supply chain. They try to keep as much inventory close
to the customers, hold some inventory at every location and store as
much raw material as possible. In such a strategy, each facility in the
supply chain optimizes its own objective with very little regard to the
impact of its decisions on other facilities in the supply chain. This typically leads to:

· High inventory levels and low inventory turns,
· High transportation costs because of the need to expedite shipments,
and
· Inconsistent service levels across locations and products.

* *Emphasize better service.* An important driver of transportation activities is typically the need to expedite products across the network due to poor service levels. When oil is cheap, this is not necessarily a huge problem. But under the new reality, there will be a significant pressure to reduce expediting costs by improving service and by better positioning inventory in the supply chain. This is also critical in the direct-to-consumer business model that is employed by many online retailers. In this case, the pressure continues to be to increase the probability of success in first-time delivery to the customer.

* *Push for tighter supply chain integration.* An important driver of inefficiencies in the supply chain is the bullwhip effect (see appendix A), which suggests that variability increases as one moves up the supply chain. That is, variability in customer demand is smaller than variability in retailer orders for the same products over the same period. Similarly, variability in retailers' orders to the distributors is smaller than variability in distributors' orders to the manufacturers. This increase in variability causes significant operational inefficiencies. For example, it reduces the ability to employ transportation capacity efficiently. This is true since high shipment variability implies that it is not clear how to plan transportation capacity. Should it be based on average or maximum shipment size? Either way, transportation cost increases. Thus, as oil prices increase, it becomes more important to reduce the bullwhip effect—that is, to reduce supply chain variability. This can be done by reducing lead times, sharing information across the various facilities in the supply chain, or strategic partnering such as vendor managed inventory (see appendix A, rule A.1). In short, the importance of tighter supply chain integration increases with escalating oil prices.

* *Rethink off-shoring strategy.* Depending on the industry and product characteristics, more and more companies need to reconsider their production sourcing strategies and even suppliers' footprint, as is discussed in the next section.

10.6   Off-shoring versus Near-shoring

In some industries, escalating and volatile oil prices are more likely to force changes in production sourcing strategies. The objective of this section is to identify product characteristics that will motivate companies to move manufacturing from off-shoring in Asia closer to market demand—such as Mexico for demand in North America and Eastern Europe for consumers in Western Europe.

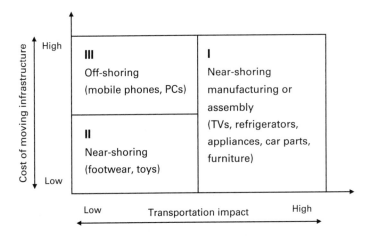

Figure 10.8
Off-shoring versus near-shoring: The effect of infrastructure and transportation

Figure 10.8 provides a framework for matching manufacturing and sourcing decisions with product and supply chain characteristics. The vertical axis provides information on the cost of moving infrastructure including manufacturing and assembly. The horizontal axis represents the transportation impact—the product's bulkiness and hence cost to transport, the ratio of transportation cost to sales price, and the impact of delivery time on the price paid by consumers (see the case of flat TVs in example 10.3).

Everything else being equal, a higher cost of moving infrastructure leads to a preference for keeping manufacturing at current locations, while a lower cost leads to an interest in near-shoring. Similarly, everything else being equal, the higher the transportation impact, the greater the value of moving from off-shoring to near-shoring.

In figure 10.8, we partition the region spanned by the two dimensions into three boxes. Box I represents bulky products where transportation plays an important role in total landed cost. Examples include furniture, appliances, flat TVs, and bulky parts for cars (such as engines). All of these products have already experienced some movement of manufacturing from off-shoring to near-shoring.

Even when transportation costs are not high (see box II) and the cost of moving the infrastructure is low, companies have started to move manufacturing closer to market demand. This is particularly true for toys, footwear, and fashion apparel.

Example 10.7

Steiff, a privately owned German manufacturing company of toys, joined the global outsourcing trend when it moved about 20 percent of production to low cost countries. The objective was to cut costs and compete on price. Recently, this toy manufacturer started moving production back to Germany, Portugal, and Tunisia because of quality problems and high transportation costs associated with manufacturing far from the key markets.[7]

Finally, box III represents industries where the cost of moving the infrastructure is high and the transportation impact is low. Examples include the supplier network of mobile phones and computers. In these cases, manufacturing of key components (such as desktop chassis, chipsets, mobile phone keypads, and semiconductors) depends on heavy infrastructure, which is difficult to move. In these situations, companies will be slow to change their production and sourcing strategies.

Another equally important driver of the decision to keep manufacturing off-shore or move to near-shore is changes in labor costs in different countries. Between 2002 and 2008, labor costs in countries such as Brazil and China have increased significantly (see table 1.1), much faster than the increase in costs in the United States and Mexico. This implies that off-shoring and outsourcing decisions that were made a few years ago may not be appropriate in the current environment.

The trade-offs between labor and transportation costs are captured by *total landed cost*, which is the effective cost of sourcing or manufacturing in one location and serving customers in another location. As observed earlier, total landed cost includes manufacturing costs, transportation costs, inventory and handling costs, duties and taxation, and the cost of finance. As transportation costs and labor costs in developing countries increase, it becomes more attractive to move manufacturing closer to demand. In fact, such a move also reduces inventory levels as it reduces lead time to key markets. We thus suggest the following rule.

Rule 10.2   *Escalating oil prices, higher labor costs in developing countries, and decline in consumer demand force more regional activities.*

For some industries, these changes may lead to more distribution centers, with each responsible for a local market. Other industries may be forced to completely change their manufacturing strategies and establish plants closer to market demand.

10.7 Summary

The increase in oil price and oil-price volatility have four important effects:

Business. Rising oil prices force companies to rethink many business strategies that have been implemented in the last two decades. Although the specifics vary from company to company, two things are certain.

· The days of indiscriminate emphasis on manufacturing in low cost countries and centralized distribution are numbered. In the new norm of rising oil prices, increased labor costs in developing countries, and moderate growth in the economies of developed countries, a more balanced mix between regional and global activities will emerge.
· The days of static supply chain strategies are over. With increasing costs and changing markets, companies must monitor and reevaluate their network and supply chain strategies on a continuous basis. Hence a switch to a more flexible supply chain strategy.

Consumers. With rising costs, business must consider whether to transfer increased costs to consumers or to absorb the increase internally and face smaller profit margins. Because some industries (such as tires and plastic) are more oil hungry, as this commodity is an important ingredient in their production processes, they are typically more willing to transfer costs to consumers. Interestingly, even food prices have increased recently. Between October 2007 and April 2008, the food Consumer Price Index (CPI) increased by 2.73 percent. Four important drivers are pushing up food prices:

· Increased supply chain costs due to escalating oil prices,
· Increased corn prices due to an increasing demand for corn-based ethanol to reduce dependency on imported petroleum,
· Increased demand from developing countries, and
· Tight supply of ingredients due to unfavorable weather conditions.

The price of corn has been especially volatile. Between October 2007 and April 2008, the price of corn rose by 56 percent. A few studies indicate that such an increase in corn price contributes less than 1 percent increase in CPI for food.[8] It is hard to explain the remaining 1.73 percent increase (2.73% minus 1%) in food CPI by an increased demand from developing countries in such a short period. Thus, our analysis indicates that the increase in food CPI is in part due to weather related supply shortage as well as higher oil prices, which increased by 40 percent between October 2007 and April 2008.

The environment. As oil prices increase, environmentally friendly supply chain strategies coincide with economically effective business strategies. Increasing cube utilization, reducing deadhead distance, and decreasing fuel consumption improve the transportation bottom line and reduce the carbon footprint. Similarly, strategies that directly focus on reducing carbon emissions typically improve transportation efficiency.

Emerging technologies. The search is on for technologies that help industry reduce energy consumption and energy costs. Here we focus on emerging technologies that can reduce transportation costs. These include onboard global positioning systems with centralized information that allows for real-time monitoring of vehicle operations, aerodynamic trac-tor-trailers, kite-assisted ocean freight, automatic tire-inflation systems, and single-wide tires (replacing the traditional two-tire systems).

Investing in emerging clean technologies or implementing operational improvements and innovation to reduce carbon footprint are all part of corporate social responsibility—an area of focus for a growing number of firms. This is examined in the next chapter.

Acknowledgment

This chapter is based on a white paper by D. Simchi-Levi, D. Nelson, N. Mulani, and J. Wright and the point of view published by R. Gosier, D. Simchi-Levi, J. Wright, and D. Brooks.[9]

Notes

1. D. Simchi-Levi, D. Nelson, N. Mulani, and J. Wright, "The Impact of Oil Price on Supply Chain Strategies: From Static to Dynamic," Massachusetts Institute of Technology, September 2008. A short version of this paper was published in the *Wall Street Journal*, September 22, 2008.

2. The case is loosely based on my experiences with several companies.

3. M. Kessler, "Sharp Takes a Gamble on New TV Plant in Mexico," *USA Today*, November 6, 2007.

4. The case is loosely based on my experiences with several companies.

5. V. Ryan, "Sucking It Up," CFO.com, 2008, available at http://cfo.com (accessed on December 23, 2009).

6. Available at http://www.es3.com (accessed on December 23, 2009).

7. G. Wiesmann, "Outsourcing Too Much to Bear for Steiff," *Financial Times*, July 14, 2008.

8. See, for example, E. Leibtag, "Corn Prices Near Record High, but What about Food Costs?," Economic Research Service, U.S. Department of Agribulture, February 2008.

9. See Simchi-Levi, Nelson, Mulani, and Wright, "The Impact of Oil Price on Supply Chain Strategies: From Static to Dynamic," Massachusetts Institute of Technology, September 2008. A short version of this paper was published in the *Wall Street Journal*, September 22, 2008; R. Gosier, D. Simchi-Levi, J. Wright, and B. A. Bentz, "Past the Tipping Point," Accenture-ILOG Point-of-View, June 2008, available at http://www.accenture.com (accessed December 23, 2009).

11

Doing Well by Doing Good

In 2006, Fonterra—New Zealand's world-leading exporter of dairy products—was faced with significant competition in local markets. In the United Kingdom, local producers ran advertisements claiming that dairy products with high food miles—those produced thousands of miles away—contribute significantly more to global warming than local produce. UK-based Dairy Crest, for example, underlined growing consumer awareness of the food-miles concept when it launched an advertising campaign comparing its locally produced products with images of Fonterra's Anchor brand butter traveling thousands of miles to Britain on a rusty ship.[1]

Fonterra took a scientific and holistic approach to the challenge. First, it demonstrated that most of the greenhouse gases emitted in the dairy-product supply chain is generated at the farming step. Second, an independent study found that New Zealand farmers used less energy producing lamb than German producers, and another study showed that producing milk in New Zealand and shipping dairy products to Britain consumed 50 percent less energy and generated 50 percent less carbon greenhouse gas than UK milk producers.[2]

Laundry detergents, to give another example, have recently been the subject of intense competition. Surprisingly, competition has been not on price but on which product is the most environmentally friendly. Major consumer product manufacturers, such as Unilever and Procter & Gamble, have introduced new concentrated laundry detergents that cost less and are more sustainable. These new detergents use 64 percent less water in their formulation than traditional counterparts, and are easier and more efficient to ship because the bottle is lighter.[3] Wal-Mart and Target both run advertisements that link saving money to saving the planet. Wal-Mart's ads note that its concentrated products reduce packaging waste—a remarkable trend for a company whose marketing has traditionally focused on everyday low-pricing and broad selection.

One theme running through these stories is that these companies believe that consumers care about social responsibility (such as global warming) and will switch from one brand to another. This is supported by recent surveys that suggest that a majority of consumers would switch to a vendor with products or services that reduce carbon emissions.[4] Of course, the missing information here is "At what price?" But the underlying message is that assuming everything else is equal, most consumers prefer greener products.

A second theme suggested by the Wal-Mart story is that sometimes (but not always) green practices lead to efficiencies and cost reduction. Indeed, the concentrated laundry detergents conserve water and are more efficient to transport.

This is not always the case. More often than not, greener performance is achieved at a cost and as a result there are difficult trade-offs to be made. The challenge faced by business executives is to identify and exploit opportunities where "doing good" is consistent with "doing well." And, when these two are not consistent, they need to apply strategies that make a greener supply chain a reality without hurting the business or even while improving its performance.

Doing good is not restricted to environmental issues. Consider Nestlé, which grew from a small company founded in 1867 in Switzerland into one of the largest global food companies. The initial business growth model was simple: establish a milk district that includes a large base of farmers, a milk processing facility, and an efficient way to produce and distribute its products to the local market. Add to the mix technical assistance to farmers about best agricultural practices, and you have a menu for success.

It was not surprising that when Nestlé entered India in 1961, it applied the same approach. It set up its first milk processing facility at Moga in the state of Punjab and provided technical assistance and education to farmers to improve milk productivity and quality. But the poor region required more assistance than what worked well in developed countries. So in Moga, Nestlé established milk collection points and chilling centers, installed farm cooling tanks, and provided the transportation to pick up milk at the farms and deliver them to the milk processing facility. In parallel, it delivered veterinary medicines and, most surprisingly, helped village women learn good dairy practices.

This program began in 1961 with 180 farmers and four milk collection centers and grew to 95,000 farmers and 1,700 centers by 2005. It provided employment, higher income, and a higher standard of living to the farmers and to the entire rural community. This business model was not a charity. It allowed Nestlé to establish a unique supply chain and generated a new stream of revenue in a challenging market.[5]

Is Nestlé's story a case of corporate social responsibility or a sound business decision? This chapter argues that it is both. That a firm can deliver social and environmental benefits when these two are embedded in the company's cultural and business vision so much so that social responsibility is barely noticeable as a distinct objective.

Rule 11.1 *Corporate social responsibility can create tangible business opportunities and value.*

The starting point in this chapter is the link between corporate social responsibility and the firm's image and brand. We argue that more often than not, social responsibility is the single most important opportunity that the firm has to create a new stream of revenue by offering new, sustainable products or by entering a new market, especially in developing countries.

The focus of the chapter then turns to reducing carbon emissions during the production and delivery of products. We illustrate that by judiciously combining environmental and operational issues, businesses can increase efficiency and create value for both the firm and society.

11.1 Corporate Social Responsibility

Corporate social responsibility is often defined as "the way that a company manages its business to positively affect society through social and environmental actions." This definition refers to community development, safety standards, and working conditions[6]—the key elements in the societal dimension—as well as supply chain decarbonization, waste management, and energy and water conservation—the key to the environmental dimension.

Not long ago, corporate social responsibility was viewed as one element in the company's image and brand. It allowed the firm to distinguish itself from the competition in an economy that had an overabundance of supply and where many products were viewed as interchangeable commodities.

Today, social responsibility goes beyond branding. It represents a radical change for businesses as they move away from pure philanthropy and mere compliance with local and international laws and toward sound business investments that create value. This value is achieved through improved efficiency, cost savings, and additional revenue streams from access to new markets and innovative new products.

Consider Coca-Cola's manual distribution centers program in Africa. The initiative provides the financing for local entrepreneurs to set up independently owned, low-cost, manually operated distribution centers. Each distribution center serves a small-scale emerging retail market where conventional distribution channels are impractical—where "truck delivery is not effective or efficient, and where outlets demand smaller, more frequent deliveries of product."[7] This business model helped Coca-Cola grow its sales and volume throughout East Africa. In Ethiopia and Tanzania, for example, Coca-Cola distributes 80 percent of its products through these distribution centers, a business model that creates jobs and generates value.[8]

This chapter's approach to corporate social responsibility is similar to the one that was used for risk management in chapter 5. Business decisions are mapped along two dimensions—expected effect on business and expected effect on society, including both environmental and social values. This is done in figure 11.1 where we classify business decisions according to these dimensions.

Box A refers to areas where what is good for business conflicts with what is good for society. Examples include operations and supply chain core activities (such as transportation, logistics, and manufacturing) that may increase carbon emission, lead to congestion, pollute natural resources, or consume limited resources (such as water or energy). This is where public policy has an important role. Indeed, polluters (such as energy providers, manufacturers, shippers, and distributors) affect the environment but do not necessarily face the direct consequences of their actions—these consequences are typically referred to as negative externalities. The role of public policy is to impose a cost structure on the polluters that will force them to take into account the effects of their activities on society and the environment.

Rule 11.2 *The role of public policy is to align company interests with social and environmental needs.*

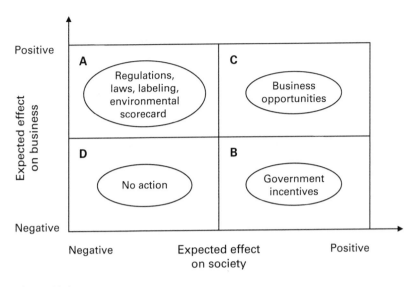

Figure 11.1
The corporate social responsibility framework

This is also where consumer-product labeling, regulated by governments or trading partners, can influence change. The Japanese government and UK retailer TESCO introduced carbon labeling that measures the emissions associated with the production and delivery of products. The assumption is that customers care about carbon emission and will force manufacturers to change their behavior through consumer buying choices.

Finally, environmental scorecards imposed by retailers play an important role. For example, in October 2005, Wal-Mart's CEO Lee Scott presented an environmental plan to reduce energy use, waste, and greenhouse-gas emissions. Wal-Mart's target is to cut greenhouse-gas emissions throughout the entire supply chain, including the supply chains of its providers, by 20 percent by 2012. For this purpose, it began in January 2008 to rate its suppliers' performance on an environmental scorecard that includes greenhouse-gas emission, transportation-cube utilization, recycled content, and renewable energy.

Box B refers to situations where a business decision may be beneficial to society or the environment but not to the firm. This is where government incentives, whose objective is to change business behavior, can make a difference—through tax incentives provided by states or (developing) countries to motivate businesses to invest in (manufacturing) infrastructure, green technology, worker education, and job training.

Box C represents situations where no incentives or regulations are required. Firms invest because these investments drive economic value. At the same time, they are able to have substantial positive effects on society. This is where the Coca-Cola and Nestlé stories belong.

Boxes B and C are directly related. Government incentives associated with box B must be designed to provide business benefits that complement social benefits. This implies that the role of government incentives is to motivate firms that make decisions with the characteristics of box B to behave as if they were in box C.

From the corporate point of view, box A is all about *operational improvements*. The focus is on measurement, best practices, and compliance. For example, Wal-Mart's sustainability initiative (described earlier) motivated its third-party logistics (3PL) provider in Canada to change the way it ships products to ten stores in Nova Scotia and Prince Edward Island from road to rail, which led to a reduction of carbon emissions by 2,600 tons. In addition, the 3PL provider converted twenty truck generators to electric power, saving about 10,000 gallons of fuel.[9]

Operational improvements (the focus of box A) are different than *business innovations* (the opportunities associated with boxes B and C). Here, the objective is to create a new value proposition that combines economic and social benefits, not mere compliance or best practices. Examples include investments in a new market segment in developing countries; the introduction of new, energy-efficient, products such as household appliances, computers, and buildings that require less energy to operate; and a new service for the poor in developed countries.

Walgreens, the drugstore retailer, has a health and wellness division that provides affordable, walk-in, seven-days-a-week healthcare services in over 300 Walgreens stores, and it plans to increase the number of its retail clinics to 2,200. The retail clinics provide diagnosis and prescriptions for common health problems and refer clients to specialists when appropriate. Walgreens is not investing in low-price healthcare services for the uninsured as a form of charity. As Walgreens' top financial executive Wade Miquelon put it, "What ends up happening is people become more loyal to Walgreens." The data suggest that he is right. With up to 30 percent of the retail clinic patients becoming new Walgreens customers, the clinics are bound to drive big business for Walgreens stores.[10]

To be successful in a way that allows business and social benefits to be indistinguishable, management must follow a four-step process:

· *Identify the opportunity.* This step is about listing and ranking opportunities that provide both business and social benefits. For box B, government incentives play an important role by generating a business opportunity in a situation where it does not exist without the incentive.

· *Analyze rigorously and systematically.* Here the focus is on available resources—labor, infrastructure, natural resources, and local industry—and on competition, market size, investment required, and tax implications.

· *Establish performance measures for success.* Avoid short term planning and focus on long-term benefits. This is important as it typically takes time to realize the potential of corporate social responsibility.

· *Implement.* Start small, monitor and review, establish best practices, and finally build scale by transferring knowledge to other regions, products, or services.

This approach to business innovation in corporate social responsibility is no different than the approach that management should take in other business investments. This is no coincidence. Succeeding in corporate social responsibility requires a similar approach to the one taken by corporations, for example, towards risk management. It needs to be embedded in the firm's core values, organizational fabric, and culture. For this purpose, management needs to distinguish between decisions associated with operational improvements and new business innovations that generate true social and economic values.

But business innovation for social responsibility has some unique characteristics. First, firms need to take a long-term perspective rather than focus on immediate shareholder benefits. Second, business and social values must be integrated so that they are indistinguishable. And finally, business innovation for social responsibility requires a departure from traditional business models, the removal of organizational barriers, and the development of an incentive and reward system that typically is different than existing ones.

The examples discussed earlier highlight these characteristics. In East Africa, Coca-Cola captured a new market by replacing traditional distribution centers with a new type of center, an approach that helped lead poor families out of poverty. Nestlé developed a new revenue stream by adding services—typically not part of Nestlé's offering—that supported the local community in Moga, India. Walgreens' story is similar. What is impressive about Walgreens is that it is addressing a challenging sector (health care) in a highly developed market (the United States). Finally, Procter & Gamble and Unilever have removed organizational boundaries between product design and operations, leading to new technologies that conserve water, reduce waste, and improve transportation.

11.2   Reducing Supply Chain Emissions

Reducing the carbon footprint of supply chain and logistics operations has become an important priority for international and national business executives. Three main factors drive this interest. First, governments are increasingly taking unilateral legislative steps to enforce compliance. The Kyoto Protocol has set loose national targets, but the European Union's Emissions Trading Scheme (EU ETS) has taken the lead, mostly in Europe, in strongly regulating emissions allowances. Second, executives link inefficiencies in the supply chain (particularly in transportation and distribution) with a high carbon footprint. The intuition is clear: the more efficient the transportation system, the lower the emissions, and vice versa. Of course, oil price is hidden behind this link. The higher the price of oil, the more executives focus on improving transportation efficiency and reducing carbon emissions.

Finally, as the Fonterra and Wal-Mart stories suggest, consumer concerns are starting to translate into a real need for new products and services. This pressure is not just being felt from consumers, but also employees, trading partners, and governments that are demanding that business take tangible steps toward becoming greener. Such pressures are escalating the issue of carbon footprint in the business agenda.

Farming, manufacturing, and logistics are large and growing contributors to carbon dioxide emissions. Logistics, for example, contributes about 5.5 percent of the total greenhouse-gas emissions generated by human activities, with transportation responsible for 89 percent and the rest attributed to warehouses and distribution facilities.[11] Manufacturing contributes around 18 percent of the total greenhouse-gas emissions.[12]

Within the transportation sector, road freight is responsible for more than half of the annual carbon dioxide emitted to the atmosphere, ocean freight is responsible for 20 percent, and rail and air for the rest.[13] Different modes of transportation have different emission efficiency, as illustrated in figure 11.2, which is based on data from Guidelines to Defra's GHG Conversion Factors,[14] with trucks generating six times higher carbon emissions than rail and long-haul air generating forty-seven times higher emissions than ocean.

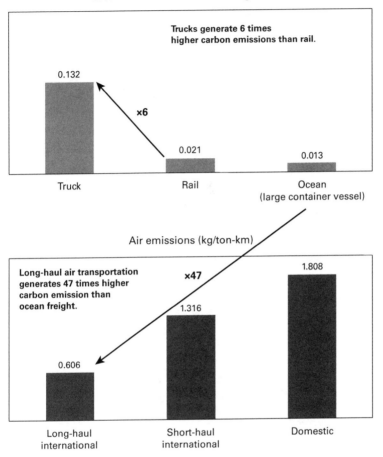

Figure 11.2
Emission efficiency by mode of transportation

Logistics is only one—and not necessarily the largest—contributor to greenhouse gas during the product lifecycle. To illustrate this point, consider the carbon footprint of a typical consumer packaged-goods product that is split among raw material (39%), manufacturing (29%), packaging (14%), distribution and logistics (12%), waste and recycling (3%), and other activities.[15]

A common mistake made by the public is to assume that local agricultural products have less of a carbon footprint than those shipped from overseas manufacturing and farming locations. This is nicely illustrated

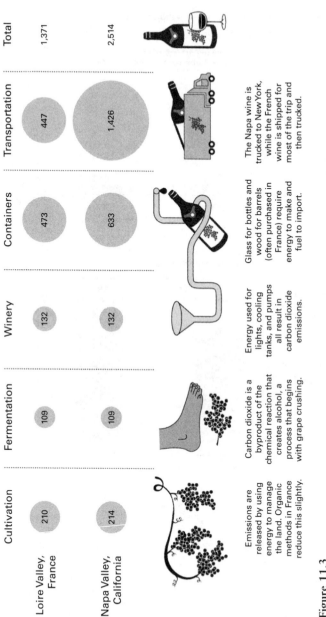

Figure 11.3
Carbon footprint for (a hypothetical) red wine sold in New York City.
Source: E. Rosenthal, "Environmental Cost of Shipping Groceries around the World," *New York Times*, April 26, 2008, C1.

by analyzing the carbon footprint of a bottle of wine sold in New York City. A typical bottle produced in the Loire Valley in France generates 45 percent less carbon dioxide than the one produced in Napa Valley, California (figure 11.3). The reason is that the French bottle is shipped mostly over the ocean while the California wine is trucked—two modes of transportation that differ significantly in carbon efficiency.

Another mistake is made by companies that try to do good by focusing only on reducing their logistics carbon footprint. Such an effort can make a difference but may miss bigger opportunities. Even worse! Just focusing on logistics, as is illustrated by the Fonterra example, without understanding the relationship with other supply chain carbon-generating activities may result in higher, not lower, levels of emission. To summarize,

---

Rule 11.3   *A holistic view of the supply chain is important for measuring and optimizing a firm's product and corporate carbon footprint.*

This rule introduces two interrelated concepts—corporate footprint and product footprint. While the former focuses on the aggregation of carbon emissions associated with all supply chain activities and across all products, the latter allocates carbon footprint to individual products depending on the product's raw materials and manufacturing and distribution activities.

So what should a company do when trying to reduce its carbon footprint? We have identified six opportunities to effectively reduce both corporate and product carbon footprints. These opportunities transcend industry sectors and product characteristics.

The first three—supply chain reconfiguration, transportation-mode optimization, and efficient packaging—are readily available, and companies in a variety of industries (including food and beverages, pharmaceuticals, high-tech, and retail) have applied them successfully.

The remaining three opportunities—recycling and waste prevention, product design for sustainability, and emerging clean technologies—can significantly reduce carbon footprint, but they require long-term planning and major efforts.

Short-Term Opportunities

We start with supply chain reconfiguration. To measure and reduce supply chain carbon footprint, it is appropriate to take a holistic view and map out all supply chain activities and their corresponding carbon-emission levels. This includes the carbon footprint that is associated with raw materials, plants, production, filling and packaging, distribution, and transportation throughout the supply chain.

Collecting the data required for the analysis is challenging since information is needed on (1) carbon emissions by fuel type, (2) average fuel efficiency by transportation mode, (3) electricity emissions by locations —different states and countries use different power-generation technologies, including coal, diesel, grid electricity, natural gas, and nuclear power, (4) electricity consumption by building characteristics such as building size, number of workers, principal activity, and year constructed, and (5) electricity consumption and emission by manufacturing processes.

This is a vast amount of data that most companies do not possess. Various resources are available, though, including software vendors that provide carbon calculators, public organizations (such as the World Resource Institute), and various government agencies. In the future, enterprise resource planning systems will likely include this information as part of their databases so that users can estimate carbon footprints by linking product bill-of-material, manufacturing, logistics, and transportation activities to carbon emissions. In this case, it will be another key performance indicator (KPI) generated by information technology.

After the supply chain's various cost components, service requirements, and carbon emissions are mapped out, an optimal supply chain configuration can be characterized to balance cost, service, and carbon footprint. For this purpose, recall rule 5.2: supply chain cost is always flat around the optimal strategy. This implies that when choosing a network strategy, it is possible to select a strategy whose total supply chain cost is close to the cost of the optimal strategy and yet is attractive from a carbon footprint point of view.

This is illustrated in figure 11.4, where we present the various cost components and supply chain carbon footprint for a (hypothetical) U.S. manufacturer of office furniture. These data are depicted as a function of the number of distribution centers. "Current design" corresponds to the existing two distribution centers. "Optimal design" reduces supply chain costs by 3 percent and cuts average distance to customers by 45 percent by adding two distribution centers. Finally, "Green design" is a supply chain design with six distribution centers. Its cost is almost identical to the optimal cost, average distance to customers is reduced by 56

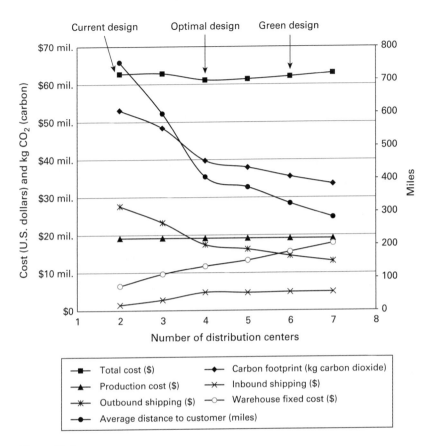

Figure 11.4
Trade-off curve between number of distribution centers, costs, service, and carbon footprint

percent, and carbon footprint is reduced by 33 percent, relative to the one associated with "Current design."

The reader may be wondering why a design with six distribution centers is greener than designs with fewer distribution centers. As the number of distribution centers increases, outbound transportation decreases (since average distance to the consumers decreases) while inbound transportation increases. This reduces greenhouse-gas emission since for this company, outbound transportation is carried out by trucks, while inbound is mostly by rail, a more efficient mode of transportation from a carbon footprint point of view. But transportation is only one contributor to this supply chain carbon footprint. The increase in the number of distribution centers implies more storage areas, and hence more energy is consumed at the distribution facilities. As figure 11.4 illustrates, the net effect is still a reduction of carbon footprint as the firm switches from a two-DC to a six-DC configuration.

A related opportunity to reduce carbon footprint is to select the mode of transportation by balancing cost, time, and emissions. To illustrate this opportunity, consider a retailer that sources its products from Asia to be sold in stores on the U.S. East Coast. Not long ago, the distribution strategy was straightforward: ship to a port on the West Coast, and truck to cities on the East Coast. When oil was cheap and carbon footprint not on the radar screen of logistics managers, this was appropriate. But with oil prices following an upward trend and with the vast difference in emission efficiency and transportation costs between ocean and truck delivery, many firms have chosen a different strategy. The alternative is to ship through the Panama canal all the way to ports on the East Coast and from there to the final destination—a cheaper and cleaner distribution strategy.

Finally, on the list of immediate opportunities for reducing carbon footprint is efficient packaging that improves utilization of transportation capacity. Efficient packaging is often achieved through better load mixing or a new packaging. Until recently, packaging was an afterthought, and little consideration was given to waste, recycling, or impact on transportation efficiency. When oil prices were low and sustainability was not yet on the consumer's mind, no one paid attention to packaging beyond its marketing role. Today packaging is at the forefront of the fight to reduce transportation costs, carbon emissions, and waste.

Long-Term Opportunities

Reducing the carbon footprint through recycling and waste prevention requires long-term planning. Recycling and waste prevention reduce carbon emissions in two stages during the product life cycle—at the product manufacturing stage and the product end-of-life stage. By far, the most important effect is achieved at the end-of-life stage.[16] Indeed, disposal of waste through incineration and landfill operations requires tremendous energy investments, and so waste prevention saves energy and reduces greenhouse-gas emissions. By contrast, recycling conserves raw material and hence reduces the carbon emissions that are associated with manufacturing. It also reduces environmental degradation and water pollution from mining, logging, and oil extraction.[17]

For all these reasons, increasing a product's life cycle will reduce carbon emissions as well. All of these require rethinking of product-design strategies.

For this purpose, we adopt the approach followed in chapter 9 for product design and focus on the interactions between the development chain and the supply chain. This approach suggests that at the product-design stage, it is important to consider the effect of different design alternatives on life-cycle cost and quality.

The same is true when considering design for sustainability. In fact, a common perception among environmentalists is that more than 80 percent of a product's environmental impact is determined at the product-design phase. Thus, at the product-design stage, there must be an emphasis on what environmentalists call the "three R" approach to design—reduce, reuse, and recycle. The best opportunity to minimize environmental impact is to reduce the amount of material used, the second is to reuse material, and the last opportunity in this hierarchy is to recycle.[18]

Thus, product life cycle, including end-of-life, must also be considered at the design stage. This allows identifying design strategies that increase the use of recycled material, reduce waste, and improve utilization of transportation capacity. Similarly, sourcing decisions need to take into account the carbon emissions that are associated with a specific component. Finally, design strategies that help consumers monitor and reduce energy consumption, are also included. Examples include energy efficient products (such as household appliances, computers, and printers) and products that enable consumers to use cold, and not hot, water (for dish washer and washing machines).

One example that illustrates this approach is Nike's program to incorporate green principles into design guidelines for developing products that include more sustainable materials and less waste. This successful initiative has led to Nike's Pegasus 25 running shoe, which uses 1.4 ounces less material than previous versions, an environmentally preferred rubber, and recycled materials.[19]

Finally, opportunities to reduce carbon footprint through emerging clean technology should not be overlooked. This includes more efficient transportation technology and new energy-efficient building to reduce energy consumption and as a result carbon footprint.

Analysis

The various carbon-reduction opportunities are summarized in table 11.1, which evaluates them along three dimensions—impact on

Table 11.1

The impact, time horizon, and effort level associated with each carbon reduction opportunity

Opportunity	Impact on corporate carbon footprint	Time horizon	Effort
Supply-chain reconfiguration	Medium to high	Medium	Medium
Transportation mode optimization	Medium	Immediate	Low
Efficient packaging	Low to medium	Immediate to medium	Low to medium
Recycling and waste prevention	Medium	Long-term	High
Product design	High	Long-term	High
Emerging clean technologies	High	Long-term	High

corporate carbon footprint, time horizon, and effort required to achieve the impact. For example, emerging clean technologies and new product designs have a high impact but require significant time and resources to realize the environmental benefits. Recycling and waste prevention have similar characteristics, but their potential impact on carbon-footprint reduction is smaller.

The impact, effort, and the time horizon for efficient packaging depend on whether efficient packaging is achieved through new product and packaging redesign or mere load mixing. Finally, supply chain reconfiguration and its close relative, transportation-mode optimization, can significantly reduce carbon footprint, but effort and time may vary. Specifically, reconfiguring the supply chain may require significant effort and will take time to achieve depending on the structure of the new network. For example, moving locations of manufacturing facilities from off-shoring to near-shoring can take a long time and demand many resources. By contrast, closing some distribution centers and opening others require less time and effort.

Undoubtedly, the specific strategy for reducing corporate and product carbon footprint varies from company to company. Yet a few principles are common to any successful sustainability strategy.

First, take a holistic view to both product design and supply chain carbon footprint. This also implies initiatives across supply chain partners to reduce waste, increase recycle content, or improve transportation efficiencies.

Second, there is no single opportunity that by itself will lead to a quantum leap reduction in carbon emission. Thus, there is a need for a portfolio of initiatives that span the entire spectrum of opportunities from product design, through transportation efficiencies, all the way to supply chain design. Similarly, there is a need for continuous improvement that empowers people to initiate and implement green opportunities—much like what is discussed in chapter 8 in the context of lean manufacturing.

Third, because this is a continuous improvement process and due to the nature of some of the opportunities, it takes time to realize the full benefits of a sustainability strategy. Be patient! An effective strategy is one where in the long-term there are both environmental and business values.

11.3   Summary

Corporate social responsibility may appear to be a form of charity, philanthropy, or mere compliance with regulations, but nothing is further from the truth. In an economy where there is an overabundance of supply and where many products are viewed as interchangeable commodities, it offers an opportunity for new revenue streams, additional efficiencies, and unique branding. To become a reality, corporate social responsibility needs to be part of the firm's business vision. This is exemplified by the India story of Nestlé, a company whose business vision is "Respected, trustworthy food, nutrition, health and wellness company," or by the East Africa story of Coca-Cola, a company whose business vision includes "be a responsible citizen that makes a difference by helping build and support sustainable communities."

Acknowledgment

Figure 11.1 is inspired by a presentation given by Nishkam Agarwal from the U.S. Environmental Protection Agency.[20] Some of the ideas covered in section 11.1 are related to those of E. M. Porter and M. R. Kramer.[21]

Notes

1. D. Patton, "Food Miles Issue No Worry to Fonterra," November 7, 2006, available at http://www.foodproductiondaily.com (accessed on December 23, 2009).

2. Ibid.

3. "Concentrated Laundry Detergents Become Latest Trend in Green Retail Packaging," September 06, 2007, available at http://www.sustainableisgood .com (accessed on December 23, 2009).

4. Accenture, "End-Consumer Survey on Climate Change," 2007, available at http://www.accenture.com (accessed on December 23, 2009).

5. M. Rolland, "Nestle India Limited: Introduction and CSR," November 29, 2006, available at http://www.nestle.in (accessed on December 23, 2009).

6. L. Kaufmann and C. Carter, "Sustainable Management in Emerging Economy Contexts," Wissenschaftliche Hochschule für Unternehmensführung (WHU) Otto Beisheim School of Management, Vallendar, Germany, available at http:// www.ism.ws (accessed on December 23, 2009).

7. J. Nelson, E. Ishikawa, and A. Geaneotes, "Developing Inclusive Business Models: A Review of Coca-Cola's Manual Distribution Centers in Ethiopia and Tanzania," Harvard University, Kennedy School of Law, Cambridge, Mass., 2009.

8. See ibid.; B. Clinton, "Creating Value in an Economic Crisis," *Harvard Business Review* (September 2009): 70–71.

9. "Wal-Mart's 'Green' Campaign Pays Off in Canada," *DCVelocity*, October 1, 2007, available at http://www.dcvelocity.com (accessed on December 23, 2009).

10. Z. Wilson, "Why Walgreens Is Building Its Own Universal Healthcare System," *Fast Company*, July 1, 2009.

11. "Supply Chain Decarbonization: The Role of Logistics and Transport in Reducing Supply Chain Carbon Emissions," report by the World Economic Forum, 2009, available at http://www.weforum.org (accessed on December 23, 2009).

12. Report by the Intergovernmental Panel on Climate Change, 2004.

13. "Supply Chain Decarbonization."

14. 2008 Guidelines to Defra's GHG Conversion Factors, available at http:// www.defra.gov.uk (accessed on December 23, 2009).

15. "Supply Chain Decarbonization."

16. "Opportunities to Reduce Greenhouse Gas Emissions through Materials and Land Management Practices," U.S. Environmental Protection Agency, Office of Solid Waste and Emergency Response, September 2009.

17. Ibid.

18. D. C. Esty and A. S. Winston, *Green to Gold: How Smart Companies Use Environmental Strategy to Innovate, Create Value, and Build Competitive Advantage* (New Haven: Yale University Press, 2006).

19. T. Herrera, "Nike: From Considered Design to Closing the Loop." This article was part of GreenBiz.com's coverage of the 2009 Business Social Respon-

sibility conference, October 19, 2009. Available at http://www.greenbiz.com (accessed on December 23, 2009).

20. N. Agarwal, "Framework Development for GSN Benefits Measurement: Public Policy Tools to Promote Corporate Environmental Performance," Paper presented at the MIT Forum for Supply Chain Innovation, March 2008.

21. E. M. Porter and M. R. Kramer, "The Link Between Competitive Advantage and Corporate Social Responsibility," *Harvard Business Review* (December 2006).

12

Barriers to Success

From my vantage point as an academic, consultant, and entrepreneur, I have observed tremendous changes in the operations and supply chain strategies employed by companies across all industries. A number of trends have emerged in the last few years—more emphasis on improving service levels, response times and satisfying customer needs; a move from a functional focus in which each area is marching to its own drum to a holistic approach to supply chain; a significant emphasis on risk-mitigation strategies to address supply and market volatility, disruptions, and globalization; and IT investments to achieve better planning, coordination, event visibility, and execution of decisions across the entire supply chain.

Taken together these trends suggest not only that operations and supply chain management have evolved, but also highlight the stage of maturity and sophistication of many organizations. All of these are of course positive developments.

But with all these positive trends, why do many companies struggle, stumble, or sometimes fail entirely in their operations strategies? My answer is that there are barriers to success—recognizing them can help an organization avoid potential problems. Unfortunately, some of these pitfalls are disguised as quite reasonable strategic goals, but when they are followed, an organization is almost guaranteed to fail or miss opportunities. This chapter reviews the top pitfalls—these are common mistakes that I refer to as the seven myths of operational excellence.

Myth 1: Reduce Costs by All Means

Some companies make cost reduction a strategic goal, particularly when times are hard and cutting costs seems to be the natural strategy to survive. This strategy violates many of the rules discussed in this book, especially the one suggesting that for certain product characteristics (such as innovative products), responsiveness, not cost reduction, is the appropriate operations strategy.

Even when cost is an important objective, companies need to balance cost with service, invest in flexibility to reduce risk, and deploy the appropriate information technology (IT) infrastructure for long-term viability and growth. Avoid these investments, and you will be taking the same journey that Ericsson's mobile division took in 2000 when it faced a supply disruption (see chapter 5). Therefore, executives need to remember an important lesson learned over the collapse of many supply chains: *Invest now, or you will pay later* (see rule 5.3).

This is exemplified by Amazon's approach to IT investments. For many years, Amazon was criticized for its low profitability, big investment in IT, and significant costs tied up with service processes. But by 2009, Amazon emerged as the largest online retailer, with high profits and superior customer service—all achieved through its investment in IT and a relentless focus on customer service.

Myth 2: Apply the Same Operations Strategy across All Products, Channels, and Customers

Companies often offer a variety of products and serve multiple customers through a number of channels. A common mistake is the deployment of one supply chain across all channels, customers, and products. Such an approach violates many of the frameworks and rules introduced in chapters 2 and 3. Products may possess different characteristics (such as innovation clock speed, demand uncertainty, and economies of scale), channels (such as retail and online) have different requirements, and customers can include a mix of individual consumers, small and midsize businesses, and large corporations, each with its own unique demand volume and response-time requirement.

Worse! It is easy to overlook this mistake. The same product may come in different forms—innovative in the online channel and functional at the retail store. Similarly, product characteristics may change during the product life cycle, starting as an innovative product and later becoming functional. All of these require product characteristics to be matched with supply chain strategies.

In my opinion, this is at the heart of some of the operational challenges that the Gap Inc. is now facing. Indeed, the firm owns three brands, Banana Republic, Gap, and Old Navy, each of which offers a different customer value proposition. Banana Republic is a specialty retailer providing a large selection of high-end fashion products; Old Navy focuses on low-cost clothing, and Gap on casual, not trendy, products. With these different value propositions, there is a need for multiple supply chains, but the Gap employs only a single one across all three brands.

By contrast, supply chain channel master Wal-Mart and fashion retailer Limitedbrands have multiple supply chains—one that flows through central distribution centers, another that ships directly to regional warehouses, and a third that ships from vendors directly to stores. HP has multiple supply chains in its printing group, each of which is associated with a specific type of customer and sales channel. The key to success is the ability to take advantage of synergies across the various supply chains—synergies in procurement, manufacturing, logistics, transportation, and order management and fulfillment.

The same is often true for mergers and acquisitions. Senior executives often target new acquisitions by focusing on revenue growth but do not pay much attention to synergies across customer value, the supply chains and operations of the two companies. Lack of synergies demand significant effort and resources to capture the potential benefits. If these efforts outpace the potential benefits, such an acquisition is doomed to fail.

To emphasize this point, consider the 1998 failed merger of Mercedes-Benz and Chrysler. Built on the promise of complementary products and geographic strength, the merger failed to "achieve global integration," according to Daimler CEO Dieter Zetsche. On the surface, the merger made strategic sense with premium vehicles from Mercedes-Benz complementing low-cost products from Chrysler and with complementary geographic strength—Mercedes-Benz mostly in Europe and Chrysler primarily in North America. The problem, of course, was that different customer value propositions of each company required completely different supply chain strategies. Indeed, Chrysler's focus on low-cost vehicles demands an efficient supply chain, quite different from the supply chain that needs to support high-end vehicles, vehicles that require focus on brand, value added service, and investment in innovative technologies.

Myth 3: Deploy the Latest and the Best Information Technology

The desire to keep up with the competition and invest in the most advanced information technology—actively encouraged by IT vendors—

seems to make a lot of sense. This is another common mistake that violates almost every IT rule introduced in chapter 6. IT investment must be driven by business needs, not the other way around.

A related mistake is to initiate a quick and comprehensive IT implementation process. On the surface, it seems there is nothing wrong with this approach. Implement quickly, and you transform your firm's IT and business environment and therefore enjoy the benefits in a relatively short period of time. However, this approach shows a lack of understanding of what IT investment entails and increases the likelihood of implementation problems and user resistance.

One reason for all these challenges is the need to adjust business processes, develop material, and build confidence. Thus, always start small by focusing on a certain geography, a single business unit, or a portion of the business that provides value and experience.

Myth 4: Ignore IT Because It Is Just Another Commodity

Seldom is technology itself a driver of improvement. Rather, it is the combination of IT infrastructure and business processes designed for supply chain integration and collaboration that allow the firm to significantly improve supply chain performance and achieve a sustainable competitive advantage.

Avoiding the seemingly conflicting myths 3 and 4 is not easy. After all, they are the basis for the IT investment dilemma described and analyzed in chapter 6. But when the challenge is addressed by following some of the principles outlined in this book's IT discussion, the benefits are enormous.

Myth 5: Invest in a Lot of Redundancy and Flexibility

Companies that focus on risk-mitigation strategies often invest in redundant and flexible processes and capacities. But redundancy and flexibility do not come free. So identifying the right trade-off between risk-mitigation strategies and cost is an important challenge.

Fortunately, a small investment in flexibility (as has been shown throughout the book) provides huge business value. That is, small investments in flexibility allow the firm to respond effectively to various types of changes and disruptions.

Similarly, the flatness of supply chain costs around the optimal low-cost strategy (see rule 5.2) suggests that many strategies can be effective.

These are strategies that provide redundant capacity without hurting supply chain costs.

The challenge is to identify how to achieve flexibility (through process, system, or product design) and where to invest in redundancy. The framework provided in this book should help companies consider these challenges by taking a systematic, rigorous approach.

Myth 6: Treat Corporate Social Responsibility as a Charity

Most executives consider initiatives to protect the environment or to provide social values as charity at best or a waste of money and time at worst. In many cases, this is far from the truth. When corporate social responsibility is aligned with business value, it generates a new stream of revenue or an innovative way to reduce costs. For example, designing products by taking into account quality and life-cycle costs can lead to efficient packaging (hence a lower transportation carbon footprint), less material (therefore waste reduction), and better recycled material. All benefit the environment and bottom line.

And finally, the most common big-impact mistake made by many executives is the following misguided goal.

Myth 7: Leave Operations to the Functional Areas of the Company

As this book's title implies, there is a direct link between the firm's value proposition and its operations strategy. Indeed, operations significantly affect the firm's revenue and profit goals precisely because of their ability to control costs, shorten response times, and improve customer service. Misalignment between the customer value proposition, typically the focus of senior executives, and operations strategy leads to higher costs and customer service problems.

By contrast, when operations executives have an equal seat beside other senior executives, natural synergies emerge. Examples include better integration of the functional areas around the firm's value proposition, alignment of new channels and products with operations strategies, a direct link between IT investments and business and operations strategies, and a risk-management culture that cuts across the entire organization. But to achieve all these benefits, senior management must be directly involved in defining goals, fostering collaboration between different units, setting performance targets, and providing incentives.

This book would be incomplete without a word of caution. Following the recommendations, frameworks, and rules described in previous chapters and avoiding the mistakes outlined in this chapter are no guarantee for success. But they can help the firm significantly increase business value and hence the likelihood of outperforming the competition. The alternative, focusing on best practices or mere inertia, is no match to the power of the innovative principles described throughout this book.

Appendix A: The Bullwhip Effect

Many suppliers and retailers have observed that although customer demand for specific products does not vary much, inventory and back-order levels fluctuate considerably across their supply chain. For instance, in examining the demand for Pampers disposal diapers, executives at Procter & Gamble noticed an interesting phenomenon.

As expected, product retail sales were fairly uniform. There is no particular day or month in which the demand is significantly higher or lower than any other. However, the executives noticed that distributors' orders placed to the factory fluctuated much more than retail sales, and P&G's orders to its suppliers fluctuated even more. This increase in variability as we travel up in the supply chain is referred to as the *bullwhip effect*.

Figure A.1 illustrates a simple three-stage supply chain—a single retailer, a single distributor, and a single manufacturer. The retailer observes customer demand and places orders to the distributor. The distributor in turn reviews its own inventory and order products from the manufacturer. The figure provides a graphical representation of orders, as a function of time, placed by different facilities and shows the increase in variability across the supply chain.

To understand how an increase in variability affects the supply chain, consider the second stage in figure A.1. The distributor receives orders from the retailer and places orders to its supplier, the manufacturer. To determine these order quantities, the distributor must forecast the retailer's demand. If the distributor does not have access to the customer's demand data, it must use orders placed by the retailer to perform its forecasting.

Since variability in orders placed by the retailer is significantly higher than variability in customer demand, as the bullwhip effect suggests, the distributor is forced to carry more safety stock than the retailer to meet the same service level as the retailer.

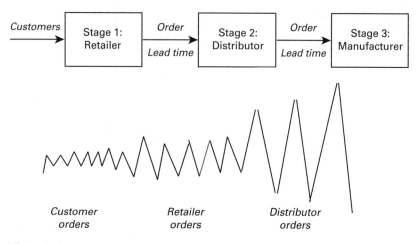

Figure A.1
A multistage supply chain and the corresponding bullwhip effect

This analysis can be carried over to the manufacturer and its own suppliers, resulting in even higher inventory levels and therefore higher costs at these facilities.

But, the bullwhip effect does not only affect inventory levels and safety stocks. It also increases manufacturing, distribution, and transportation costs. This is true, since effectively allocating and managing resources (such as equipment and machines, workforce and transportation capacity) is difficult when variability is high.

Thus, it is important to identify techniques and tools that will help control the bullwhip effect—that is, address the increased variability in the supply chain. For this purpose, the main drivers contributing to increases in variability in the supply chain need to be understood:

1. *Demand forecasting* Traditional inventory management techniques practiced at each level in the supply chain lead to the bullwhip effect. The connection between forecasting and the bullwhip effect can be explained by a review of inventory control strategies in supply chains. An attractive policy used at each stage of the supply chain is the *periodic review policy*, where the inventory policy is characterized by a single parameter—the base-stock level. Each supply chain stage (retailer, distributor, and manufacturer) determines a target inventory level (the base-stock level), and during each review period, the inventory is reviewed and the facility orders enough to raise inventory to the base-stock level.

The base-stock level is typically set equal to the average demand during lead time (more precisely, lead time plus review period) plus the *safety stock* (the amount of inventory carried to protect against changes in demand during lead time). Typically, managers use *standard forecast smoothing techniques* to estimate average demand and demand variability, and these data are used to determine the safety stock and the base-stock level. An important characteristic of all forecasting techniques is that as more data are observed, the more the estimates of average and variability in customer demand can be modified. Since safety stock and base-stock level depend on these estimates, the user is forced to change order quantities, thus increasing variability.

2. *Lead time*   The increase in variability is magnified with increasing lead time. To understand the link between lead time and variability, observe that to calculate safety stock and base-stock levels, we multiply estimates of the average and standard deviations of the daily customer demands by the lead time plus the review period. Thus, with longer lead times, a small change in the estimate of demand variability implies a significant change in safety stock and base-stock levels, leading to a significant change in order quantities. This leads to an increase in variability.

3. *Batch ordering*   If the retailer uses batch ordering, then the distributor will observe a large order, followed by several periods of no orders, followed by another large order, and so on. Thus, the distributor sees a distorted and highly variable pattern of orders.

4. *Price fluctuation*   Price fluctuation can also lead to the bullwhip effect. If prices fluctuate, retailers often attempt to *stock up* when prices are lower. This is accentuated by the prevailing practice in many industries of offering promotions and discounts at certain times or for certain quantities. This practice, referred to as *forward buying*, implies that retailers purchase large quantities during distributors' and manufacturers' discount and promotion times and order relatively small quantities at other time periods.

5. *Inflated orders*   Inflated orders placed by retailers during shortage periods tend to magnify the bullwhip effect. Such orders are common when retailers and distributors suspect that a product will be in short supply and therefore anticipate receiving supply proportional to the amount ordered. When the period of shortage is over, the retailer goes back to its standard orders, leading to all kinds of distortions and variations in demand estimates.

6. *Lack of information sharing*   If customer demand information is not shared among all supply chain stages, then each stage must use information about orders received from the previous supply chain stage. Since these orders have much higher variability than customer demand, forecast accuracy is poor, resulting in more safety stock, a higher base-stock level, and even higher variability in orders to upstream facilities.

Although there are many causes for the bullwhip effect, strategies are available for reducing its magnitude. These include reducing uncertainty, reducing the variability of the customer demand process, reducing lead times, and engaging in strategic partnerships. These issues are discussed briefly below.

1. *Reduction of uncertainty*   One of the most frequent suggestions for decreasing or eliminating the bullwhip effect is to reduce uncertainty throughout the supply chain by sharing customer demand information— that is, by providing each stage of the supply chain with complete information on actual customer demand.

Even if each stage uses the same demand data, each may still employ different forecasting methods and different buying practices, both of which may contribute to the bullwhip effect. In addition, even when each stage uses the same demand data, the same forecasting method, and the same ordering policy, the bullwhip effect will continue to exist—at a lower level—because of the need to apply forecast.

2. *Reduction of variability*   The bullwhip effect can be diminished by reducing the variability inherent in the customer demand process. For example, if the variability of the customer demand seen by the retailer can be reduced, then even if the bullwhip effect occurs, the variability of the demand seen by the wholesaler will also be reduced.

The variability of customer demand can be reduced, for example, through the use of an everyday-low-pricing (EDLP) strategy. When a retailer uses EDLP, it offers a product at a single consistent price rather than offering a regular price with periodic price promotions. By eliminating price promotions, a retailer can eliminate many of the dramatic shifts in demand that occur with these promotions. Therefore, everyday-low-pricing strategies can lead to much more stable (that is, less variable) customer demand patterns.

3. *Lead time reduction*   The previous analysis indicates that lead times magnify the increase in variability due to demand forecasting. Therefore, lead time reduction can significantly reduce the bullwhip effect throughout a supply chain.

Lead times typically include two components—order lead times (the time it takes to produce and ship the item) and information lead times (the time it takes to process an order). This distinction is important since order lead times can be reduced through the use of cross-docking, while information lead time can be reduced through the use of electronic data interchange (EDI).

4. *Strategic partnerships*   The bullwhip effect can be eliminated by engaging in any of a number of strategic partnerships. These strategic partnerships change the way that information is shared and inventory is managed within a supply chain, possibly eliminating the impact of the bullwhip effect. For example, in vendor managed inventory (VMI), the manufacturer manages the inventory of its product at the retailer outlet and therefore determines for itself how much inventory to keep on hand and how much to ship to the retailer in every period. Therefore, in VMI, the manufacturer does not rely on the orders placed by a retailer, thus avoiding the bullwhip effect entirely.

These key insights can be summarized with the following rule:

Rule A.1   *Information sharing, lead time reduction, and strategic partnering reduce variability in the supply chain.*

Appendix B: Rules

Rule 2.1 The operations strategy that a company deploys must be driven by the value proposition that the firm provides to its customers.

Rule 2.2 Functional and innovative products typically require different supply chain strategies.

Rule 2.3 Different channels may require different supply chain strategies.

Rule 2.4 Competition on price requires tight control of supply chain costs.

Rule 2.5. Differentiation through after-sale service requires specialized supply chain capabilities.

Rule 2.6 Improved customer experience requires a higher level of supply chain excellence.

Rule 3.1 Aggregate forecasts are always more accurate than individual forecasts.

Rule 3.2 The appropriate supply chain strategy—push, pull, or push-pull—is driven by demand uncertainty and economies of scale.

Rule 3.3 Lead times are drivers of the appropriate supply chain strategy.

Rule 3.4 The sales channel determines the manufacturing and distribution strategies.

Rule 4.1 The higher the supply and price risks, the more important it is to invest in procurement flexibility—the ability to effectively and efficiently switch from one supplier to another.

Rule 4.2 Effective supply contracts help firms achieve global optimization by allowing buyers and suppliers to share risks and potential benefits.

Rule 5.1 Integrate risks into operational and business decisions.

Rule 5.2 Supply chain cost is always flat around the optimal strategy.

Rule 5.3   Invest now, or pay later: firms need to invest in flexibility, or they will pay the price later.

Rule 6.1   Enabling, supporting, and enforcing a business strategy are the objectives of IT investments.

Rule 6.2   IT should be used not only to monitor current supply chain performance but also to predict what is likely to happen if no corrective action is taken.

Rule 6.3   IT investments need to be accompanied by similar and considerable investments in the appropriate business processes.

Rule 6.4   A typical organization needs a portfolio of IT platforms.

Rule 6.5   Start simple, and add complexity later.

Rule 6.6   Do not fall in love with technology capabilities.

Rule 7.1   A small investment in flexibility can significantly reduce total supply chain costs.

Rule 7.2   A long chain is preferred when designing the manufacturing network for flexibility.

Rule 7.3   Variability degrades the performance of the supply chain while flexibility improves its performance.

Rule 8.1   The Toyota production system embraces flexibility.

Rule 8.2   To achieve the maximum line throughput, balance the production line by achieving the same worker utilization.

Rule 8.3   Cross-training, properly implemented, equalizes worker utilization.

Rule 8.4   Small levels of cross-training achieve most of the benefits of full-skill cross-training.

Rule 8.5   Variability degrades production-line performance.

Rule 9.1   Modular product architecture is important when flexibility is required.

Rule 10.1   A small investment in system flexibility can help a firm reduce the effects of oil price increases or oil price volatility.

Rule 10.2   Escalating oil prices, higher labor costs in developing countries, and decline in consumer demand force more regional activities.

Rule 11.1   Corporate social responsibility can create tangible business opportunities and value.

Rule 11.2   The role of public policy is to align company interests with social and environmental needs.

Rule 11.3   A holistic view of the supply chain is important for measuring and optimizing a firm's product and corporate carbon footprint.

Rule A.1   Information sharing, lead time reduction, and strategic partnering reduce variability in the supply chain.

Index